THE GREEK ISLANDS
Genius Loci

Author's acknowledgements

This series of twenty books covering the Aegean Islands is the fruit of many years of solitary dedication to a job difficult to accomplish given the extent of the subject matter and the geography involved. My belief throughout has been that only what is seen with the eyes can trustfully be written about; and to that end I have attempted to walk, ride, drive, climb, sail and swim these Islands in order to inspect everything talked about here. There will be errors in this text inevitably for which, although working in good faith, I alone am responsible. Notwithstanding, I am confident that these are the best, most clearly explanatory and most comprehensive artistic accounts currently available of this vibrant and historically dense corner of the Mediterranean.

Professor Robin Barber, author of the last, general, *Blue Guide to Greece* (based in turn on Stuart Rossiter's masterful text of the 1960s), has been very generous with support and help; and I am also particularly indebted to Charles Arnold for meticulously researched factual data on the Islands and for his support throughout this project. I could not have asked for a more saintly and helpful editor, corrector and indexer than Judy Tither. Efi Stathopoulou, Peter Cocconi, Marc René de Montalembert, Valentina Ivancich, William Forrester and Geoffrey Cox have all given invaluable help; and I owe a large debt of gratitude to John and Jay Rendall for serial hospitality and encouragement. For companionship on many journeys, I would like to thank a number of dear friends: Graziella Seferiades, Ivan Tabares, Matthew Kidd, Martin Leon, my group of Louisianan friends, and my brother Iain— all of whose different reactions to and passions for Greece have been a constant inspiration.

This work is dedicated with admiration and deep affection to Ivan de Jesus Tabares-Valencia who, though a native of the distant Andes mountains, from the start understood the profound spiritual appeal of the Aegean world.

McGILCHRIST'S GREEK ISLANDS

14. CHIOS
WITH OINOUSSES & PSARA

GENIUS LOCI PUBLICATIONS
London

McGilchrist's Greek Islands 14 Chios with Oinousses & Psara
First edition

Published by Genius Loci Publications
54 Eccleston Road, London W13 0RL

Nigel McGilchrist © 2010
Nigel McGilchrist has asserted his moral rights.

ISBN 978-1-907859-18-2

A CIP catalogue record of this book is available from the British Library.

The author and publisher cannot accept responsibility or liability for
information contained herein, this being in some cases difficult to verify
and subject to change.

Layout and copy-editing by Judy Tither

Cover design by Kate Buckle

Maps and plans by Nick Hill Design

Printed and bound in Great Britain by TJ International Ltd, Padstow, Cornwall

The island maps in this series are based on the cartography of
Terrain Maps
Karneadou 4, 106 75 Athens, Greece
T: +30 210 609 5759, Fx: +30 210 609 5859
terrain@terrainmaps.gr
www.terrainmaps.gr

This book is one of twenty which comprise the complete, detailed
manuscript which the author prepared for the *Blue Guide: Greece,
the Aegean Islands* (2010), and on which the *Blue Guide* was
based. Some of this text therefore appears in the *Blue Guide*.

A NOTE ON THE TEXT & MAPS

Some items in the text are marked with an asterisk: these may be monuments, landscapes, curiosities or individual artefacts and works of art. The asterisk is not simply an indication of the renown of a particular place or item, but is intended to draw the reader's attention to things that have a uniquely interesting quality or are of particular beauty.

A small number of hotels and eateries are also marked with asterisks in the *Practical Information* sections, implying that their quality or their setting is notably special. These books do not set out to be guides to lodging and eating in the Islands, and our recommendations here are just an attempt to help with a few suggestions for places that have been selected with an eye to simplicity and unpretentiousness. We believe they may be the kind of places that a reader of this book would be seeking and would enjoy.

On the island maps:

∴   denotes a site with visible prehistoric or ancient remains

☦   denotes a church referred to in the text
(on Island Maps only rural churches are marked)

✝   denotes a monastery, convent or large church referred to in the text

🏰   denotes a Byzantine or Mediaeval castle

♜   denotes a Genoese watch-tower

⛲   denotes an important fresh-water or geothermic spring

⛴   denotes a harbour with connecting ferry services

Road and path networks:

-     a continuous line denotes a metalled road
or unsurfaced track feasible for motors

-     a dotted line denotes footpath only

CONTENTS

Chios   **9**
  Chios town and the Kampos area   22
  Central Chios and *Nea Moni*   53
  Southern Chios and the Mastic Villages   74
  Northwest of the island   106
  Northeast of the island   114

Oinousses   **137**

Psara   **150**

Glossary   **166**

Index   **172**

Maps
  Chios and Oinousses   8
  Psara   150

Plans
  Chios town   24
  Kampos   48
  Nea Moni   56
  Emporeio, ancient sites   80
  Mesta   98

Illustrations
  Incised, Hellenistic funerary *stele* from Chios 40
  Nea Moni, elevation   60

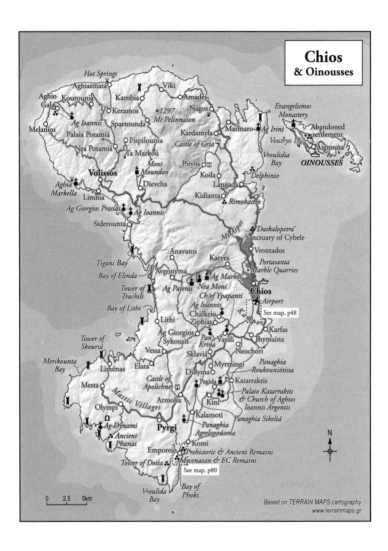

Chios
& Oinousses

Hot Springs
Aghiasmata
Aghio   Kourounia   Viki   Amades
Gala
Keramos   Nagos
Kambia
Ag Ioannis   *1297   Evangelismos
Spartounda   Mt Pelinnaion   Monastery
Melanios   Kardamyla   Marmaro   Ag Irini   Abandoned
Palaia Potamiá   Castle of Gria   Voutryo   settlement
Nea Potamiá   Ta Markoú   Pityos   Aignousa
Pispilounta   OINOUSSES
Vrouliída
Moni   Koila   Delphinio   Bay
Volissos   Moundon   Langada
Dievcha   Kidianta   Rimokastro
Aghía
Markélla
Limniá
Ag Giorgios Prasiás   'Daskalopetra'
Ag Ioannis   Sanctuary of Cybele
Siderounta   Vrontados
Portasanta
Anavatos   Karyes   Marble Quarries
Tigani Bay   Avgonyma   Ag Markos
Bay of Elinda   Nea Moni
Ag Pateras   Ch of Ypapanti   Chios
Tower of   Ag Ioannis   Airport
Trachili   Chalkeio   See map, p48
Bay of Lithi   Ziphias
Lithi   Pan.   Karfas
Ag Giorgios   Krina   Vavili   Thymiana
Tower of   Sykousis   Neochori
Skouriá   Vessa   Sklaviá   Panaghia
Merikounta   Elata   Didyma   Myrmingi   Roukouniótissa
Bay   Limenas   Pagida   Katarraktis
Mesta   Castle of   Palaio Katarraktis
Apolichnes   Kini   & Church of Aghios
Olympi   Armolia   Ioannis Argentis
Ag Dynami   Kalamoti   Panaghia Sikeliá
Ancient   Pyrgi   Panaghia
Phanai   Agrelopoúsena
Komi
Emporeió   Prehistoric & Ancient Remains
Tower of Dotia   Mycenaean & EC Remains
See map, p80
Vrouliída   Bay of
Bay   Phoki

Mastic Villages

N

0   2.5   5km

Based on *TERRAIN MAPS* cartography
www.terrainmaps.gr

CHIOS

Grand and solitary, rich in architecture and flora, but tinged with a note of tragedy that lingers from the events of its long and complex history, Chios is—perhaps more than any island in the Aegean—a world to itself. It is separated by wide, open waters from its nearest neighbours—55 nautical miles from Samos with whom relations were cool since Antiquity, and a comparable distance from Lesbos with whom its links historically were few. It has acquired over time a proud independence and self-sufficiency; yet it is still intensely Greek in feel. Both its mountainous profile and its character are aquiline, and there is a harder edge to its landscape which contrasts markedly with that of its biggest neighbour: where there is a femininity to Lesbos in the expanses of olive-groves and sheltered, almost landlocked, gulfs, Chios has an open, rugged and dramatic coast with some of the wildest highlands of the Aegean in its interior. Lyric Sappho was from Lesbos; Chios claims epic Homer.

Of the wealthy ancient city, with its walls of polychrome marble, which was shown to Cicero when he visited the island, little remains to be seen today; but a sense of its artistic individuality and political activity is vividly evoked in the city's Archaeological Museum. The island has an unbroken history of excellence in the visual arts. An architectural renaissance followed on from the building of the monastic complex of *Nea Moni*, by the Emperor in Byzantium in the early 11th century. It dates from only a few decades earlier than the Monastery of St John on Patmos, but the two buildings could not be more different. Stylised and sophisticated, with rich decoration and a cleverly modulated and dramatic interior, *Nea Moni* influenced over the following centuries the building of a number of other unusual churches around the island—Aghii Apostoli in Pyrgi, and the rural churches of the Panaghia Krina and Panaghia Sikelia—all of which are later meditations and variations on the great 11th century church. The refined mosaics of *Nea Moni*—large parts of which somehow survived the Turkish devastations of 1822 and the earthquake of 1881—are amongst the most important in Greece. The smaller churches have important paintings—those especially from Panaghia Krina, now displayed in Chios town, which bear interesting comparison with their contemporaries in Italy. But the variety of painting on Chios does not end at the Middle Ages: in the evocative ruins of the *Moni Moundon*, in a remote valley of the central north of the island, is a curious cycle of 19th century 'naïf-Byzantine' paintings; and, most unexpected of all, in the tiny chapel of the Ypapanti (the Purification of the Virgin) south of Chora, are the enchanting murals painted in 1963 by the Hawaiian artist, Juliette May Fraser, and given as a gift to the villagers of Vavili.

Unique to the south of Chios are the house-fronts decorated in grey and white geometric designs in *sgraffito* technique which constitute such an attractive aspect of the village of Pyrgi, and others of the 'Mastic Villages'. Unique also is the planned, fortified design of these mediaeval villages, densely built within walls around a central tower; unique to Chios is the cultivation and harvesting of mastic gum from the trees, which has never been successfully replicated anywhere else in the Mediterranean; and unique are the lengths to which the Genoese overlords of the 14th and 15th centuries went to protect their monopoly on mastic trade—fortifying the whole island with a circuit of 50 watchtowers, fortresses and lookout posts, as if the island itself were just one big castle in the sea. Like Genoa, the city of Chios is hemmed between the mountains and the water; the Genoese must immediately have felt at home here. They settled and slowly became Greek over the centuries, continuing to run the economy of the island together with the local Greek families, long after it came under Ottoman administration—with the firm and cautious grip for which the Genoese are known in Italy today. In the garden area to the south of the city, known as Kampos ('*Il Campo*'), they built stone villas, farmsteads and orchards to classicising designs, out of a warm red local stone, creating one of the most beautiful and historic suburbs in Greece. The same families, rich from trade and shipping, endowed their city with libraries and institutions of learning. Chios was an elegant, civilised and peaceful city, when it was suddenly dragged undeservingly into a vortex of carnage and destruction in 1822. This was immortalised in the European imagination by Delacroix's tragic painting of the *Massacre of Chios*. Something of the background to those events is explained in the epilogue to the Chios section of this book.

In spite of the loss of some areas of forest, flora, birds and butterflies are abundant and varied on Chios. The island is rich in herbs, honey, and in flavours that range from the cleansing pungency of mastic to that of the aromatic samphire which grows on the island's cliffs and animates the salads served at its tables.

HISTORY

An exceptional fall of snow on the island accompanied the birth of Chios, the son of Poseidon, after whom the island was subsequently named, according to legend. But Isidoros the historian adds that the name 'Chios' is actually of Phoenician origin, meaning 'mastic'. This is very likely true, since many of the Aegean Island names are of Phoenician rather than Greek origin.

Human settlement appears to have begun on Chios in the 6th millennium BC. Several prehistoric sites have been located near the north and south coasts. The earliest is the cave-settlement at Aghio Gála in the extreme northwestern corner; but the most extensively explored is at Emporeio on the southeast coast, where habitation was continuous from the Late Neolithic (5th millennium BC) through to the first destruction or abandonment of the site at the end of the Myceneaean era in the 12th century BC. The site, however, proved to be of greater longevity: it was re-settled in early historic times and remained occupied through until the Early Christian period. Ionians from *Histiaia* in Euboea migrated to Chios and colonised the island under the leadership of Amphicles who is mentioned as the island's first king. It was in this period—the

9th century BC—that the site of the city of Chios was also settled.

Under what may have been an enlightened oligarchy enshrined in a mid-6th century constitution, the city came to prominence rapidly as a wealthy trading centre, always to some extent in competition with *Erythrae* on the mainland opposite. It traded its goods and its renowned wine far into the Black Sea and west into the Mediterranean, and it appears to have participated in the creation of the Greek trade-*emporion* of Naucratis in the Nile Delta. It was also one of the earliest Greek cities to engage in the slave trade—a source of considerable wealth to the island, as it was also later to be to Delos. The Chiots appear to have had more domestic slaves than any other Greek state except for Sparta by the end of the 5th century BC. The city's quality of life became proverbial, giving rise to expressions such as 'the Chian life' or 'Chian laughter'. Thucydides (*Peloponnesian War*, VIII. 24) meanwhile extolled the prosperity and prudence of the islanders.

Chios was one of the twelve cities which comprised the Ionian League, whose common sanctuary and meeting place was the 'Panionium' on the promontory of Mycale opposite Samos. Here, the *Panionia* or great national assembly of the confederacy was held. The League was a vital strategic union which gave rise to commercial power, a high standard of living, and a ferment of cultural and intellectual activity among its members. Though not uninflenced by the close proximity of a great and ancient Persian cultural presence, this activity had a new, free-thinking and importantly Greek character to it. Many of the greatest thinkers and artists of the Archaic and Early Classical periods hailed from the cities of the confederacy—the philosophers Thales of Miletus, Heraclitus of Ephesus, and Pythagoras of Samos, the poet Anacreon of Teos, and the painters Apelles of Colophon, Zeuxis of Heracleia (Miletus), and Parrhasius of Ephesus. On Chios, in particular, was a celebrated school of sculpture, in which Pliny cites Achermos and his family as important masters; and according to Herodotus (*Histories* I. 25), Glaucus (fl. 490 BC) of Chios is said to have invented the art of soldering metals. The tragic poet Ion, the historian Theopompus, and the sophist Theocritus were also from Chios. But the island's greatest claim of all was to have given birth to Homer.

Out of pragmatism Chios established good relations with Croesus, King of Lydia between 560–546 BC, but it

later came under the control of Harpagus, the general of
Cyrus, King of Persia. When, in 499 BC, the Ionians re-
volted against Persian domination, instigated primarily
by Aristagoras, Governor of Miletus, Chios played an important role, sending 100 ships to the Battle of Lade in
494 BC and fighting with notable valour. The Greek fleet
was defeated, Miletus was sacked and Chios appears also
to have suffered some destruction. Later, after the final
defeat of the Persian invasions, Chios encouraged Athens
to set up the Delian League, and remained a member of
it until 412 BC. Thucydides implies (*Peloponnesian War*,
III. 10) that Lesbos and Chios saw themselves in a privi-
leged position in the League, as allies of Athens rather
than as subordinates as the other members—including
even Miletus—were. At first, Chios remained a loyal ally
of Athens—even through difficult times; but in 412 BC,
joined by Alcibiades who had defected to Sparta and by
other Ionian cities including Miletus, Teos and Mytilene,
the island broke free from Athens. The uprising failed,
and as a consequence the Athenians captured Oinousses
and established a naval stronghold at Delphinio on the
northeast coast. When Athens was subsequently defeated
by Sparta at the battle of Aigos Potami, Sparta took con-

trol of Chios, destroyed her ship-yards and expropiated her fleet.

In 383 BC, Chios was once again allied with Athens and five years later joined the Second Athenian Confederacy. With the aid of King Mausolus of Halicarnassus it seceded in 357 BC and finally gained its autonomy. In the febrile world of the 4th century BC, autonomy was virtually impossible for a city of any wealth to maintain, and Chios was divided between pro-Persian and pro-Macedonian factions. The island was captured by a general of Alexander the Great in 333 BC. It appears from the preserved and engraved epistle from Alexander to the people of the island (exhibited in the Archaeology Museum in Chios) that he restored the democratic regime, imposed a penalty of 20 triremes, and ordered the return of political exiles. This restored the island's trade for a substantial period and helped it to grow wealthy once again—something which attracted the unwanted attention of the infamous Roman Legate and Pro-Quaestor, Verres, who pillaged the island. Chios, as an ally of Rome in the war with Antiochus, suffered a yet worse destruction in 86 BC at the hands of Zenobios, the general of Mithridates VI: it is recorded that the Chians were delivered up to their own slaves, to be carried away captive to Colchis. Athenaeus considered this a just punishment for their wickedness in first introducing the slave-trade into Greece. From this, the ancient proverb arose, 'The Chian hath bought himself a master.' After the re-capture of the island by Sulla, Chios was once again given its independence, which was initially respected by the Roman Emperors. After the earthquake of 17 BC, Tiberius, who visited the island twice, contributed towards its rehabilitation. With the administrative reforms of Diocletian, Chios (c. 300 AD) became part of the *Provincia Insularum*.

St Paul appears to have visited the island (Acts XX. 15) in 58 AD. By the 4th century a small Christian community was well-established on the island, whose patron saint was St Isidore, a 3rd century Roman military martyr of the reign of Decius. Imperial Byzantine interest in the building of *Nea Moni* in 1042, brought an architectural and religious golden age to the island. This period was briefly interrupted by occupation at the hands of the Turkish emir of Smyrna, Çaka, or 'Zachas', until the island was freed again in 1092 by Alexander Comnenus. In 1125 the Venetians removed the relics of St Isidore to Venice, and in 1172 the island was taken by Doge Vitale Michiel. The partition of Byzantine territories in 1204 after the Fourth

Crusade awarded Chios to the Latin emperor in Constantinople, who proved unable to hold it. The treaty of Nymphaion in 1261 put it officially under Genoese control for the first time: by the middle of the 14th century, Genoese domination of the whole island was secure under the aegis of the Giustiniani family. In 1344 they formed the 'Moana', a chartered company which administered the island and was responsible for its defence.

Chios gained considerable wealth once again through the trade in mastic resin. It was to favour and protect the trade of this valuable product that the Genoese embarked on an impressive project of fortifying the whole island with castles and towers, and securing, as fortified settlements, the villages that produced the mastic crop. Wine was also an important element of the economy as it had been in antiquity. As early as 1513 an English *chargé d'affaires* was appointed to look after the Levant Company which was engaged in trading cloth for wine. The Turks captured Chios from the Genoese in 1566. Under Ottoman dominion the island enjoyed commercial priveleges and some autonomy, in acknowledgement of the importance of its mastic trade which was now managed from Istanbul.

At the beginning of the War of Greek Independence in 1821 the Samians fatally pressed the undecided Chiots to join them in their revolt against Turkish dominion. In 1822 the Turks—alarmed by the prospect of losing their most valuable possession in the Aegean—inflicted a dreadful and disproportionate vengeance: it is said that they massacred over 20,000 islanders and deported or enslaved twice that number. (*See Epilogue to this section, pp. 126–132.*) Only the Mastic Villages were spared. The brutality of the reprisals caused dismay throughout Europe. Eugène Delacroix—then only 24 years old—immortalised the incident in his grand and tragic painting, *Le Massacre de Scio*, which was exhibited in the Grand Salon less than two years later.

Chios never fully recovered from the events of 1822. In June of the same year the Greek admiral Constantine Kanaris from Psará avenged his compatriots by destroying the Turkish flagship with its commander, Kara Ali, aboard. What was left of the city was again ravaged: but those Chiots who had managed to escape the April massacre had already fled abroad. The more fortunate of the refugees from the island later made a name for themselves as merchants in London, Liverpool, Manchester, Paris, Marseille,

Trieste, Livorno, Palermo, Odessa, Alexandria, and even in India. Fewer than 60 years later, a powerful earthquake in 1881 killed more than 3,500 islanders, and again destroyed a large amount of the city and the island's architectural heritage.

In 1912 the island was liberated by the Greek fleet. The rugged and hidden spaces of the island's interior facilitated the endurance of a fierce resistance to German occupation during the Second World War. Chios has a millennial tradition of seamanship, and a number of Greece's most successful and best known shipping families, which still dominate the international mercantile navy, originate from the island.

The guide to the island has been divided into five sections:
- *Chios town and the Kampos area*
- *Central Chios and Nea Moni*
- *Southern Chios and the Mastic Villages*
- *Volissós and the Northwest of the island*
- *Kardámyla and the Northeast of the island*

CHIOS TOWN & THE KAMPOS AREA

The setting of the city of Chios, between the island's eastern shore and the limestone rockfaces of the mountains that rise steeply to between 700 and 800m behind, is dramatic—and must have been particularly beautiful in Antiquity. The wide, semicircular port looked straight into the heartland of Asia Minor, 5 nautical miles away, across a mostly tranquil stretch of sea. The western hills provided ample fresh water in springs which are still used today (e.g at Panaghia Voïthias), while the lower hills to north and south supplied the city with the building materials it needed—the beautiful pink and blue-grey, decorative marble, **Marmor Chium**, known later as 'Portasanta', which came from the hill-top quarries just to the northwest of the city-centre at 'Latomi' (*see pp. 34–35*), and the orange and red, 'poros' limestones from near Thymianá to the south of the city. Chios must have been one of the few cities in the Ancient world whose walls were of coloured stone. Pliny relates how Cicero was shown this with pride by the people of Chios, but that their distinguished visitor remained stoically unimpressed (*Nat. Hist.*, XXXVI, 5. 46). The city's 'garden'—the fertile, well-watered plain, still referred to today as '*Kampos*' ('meadow')—extended immediately to the south along the coast; indeed the whole southeast corner of the island was a gentle landscape of well-watered valleys, ideal for the cultivation of olives and vines which produced some of the most renowned wines of the Ancient Greek world.

THE TOWN CENTRE

On arrival today, however, the modern appearance of the harbour-front does no service to what was formerly one of the most elegant and sophisticated towns in the Aegean: the severe earthquake of 1881 destroyed nearly all of the grand architecture of the port. The gracious streets of neoclassical houses in Vaporia and Vrontado on Syros, which were built by émigrés from Chios in the image of their city of origin, give some distant idea of how this harbour-front must have appeared before the earthquake.

The true heart of the town lies a few blocks inland, around the public gardens and the **Plateia Vounáki** (officially known as **Plateia Plastíra**): when the Judas Trees are in flower here and along the borders of some of the principal streets, such as Koundouriotou Street, the town presents a wholly different aspect. The area of narrow streets just to the south of the gardens and west of the

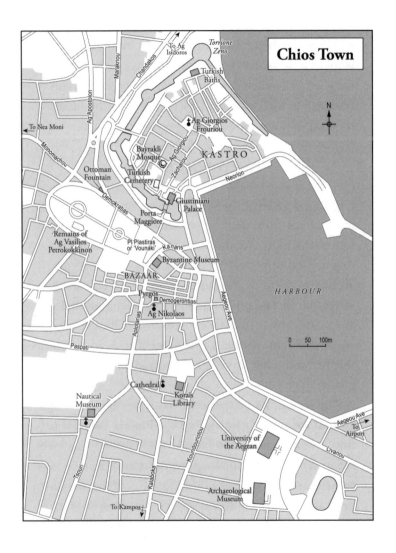

Chios Town

To Ag
Isidoros

Torrione
Zeno

Turkish
Baths

Chandakos

Marakiou

Ag Apostolon

To Nea Moni

Monomachou

Ag Giorgios
Frouriou

Bayrakli
Mosque

Ag Giorgiou

KASTRO

Zachariou

Neorion

N

Ottoman
Fountain

Turkish
Cemetery

Demokratias

Giustiniani
Palace

Porta
Maggiore

Remains of
Ag Vasilios
Petrokokkinon

Pl Plastiras
or 'Vounaki'

Kanaris

Byzantine Museum

BAZAAR

Aplotarias

Pyrgos
Demogerontias

Ag Nikolaos

HARBOUR

Aegeou Ave

Paspati

0   50   100m

Cathedral

Korais
Library

Nautical
Museum

University of
the Aegean

Aegeou Ave

To
Airport

Livanou

Koundouriotou

Kalaboka

Tsouri

Archaeological
Museum

To Kampos

central harbour-front, is the old **bazaar**: here, amongst a wide variety of tradesman's workshops, can be bought some of the island's specialties—the mastic products, good ouzo and local wine, a multifarious production of kinds of bread, and the wild ****samphire** ('*kritamo*'), which is such a distinctive and aromatic element in the island's salads.

In this area is one of the few mediaeval, civil buildings to have survived in the city—a small, red-stone *pyrgos* (now a café) at the junction of Demogerontías Street with the alleyway of Magaziótissas Street, opposite the little chapel of Aghios Nikolaos. The building's corner corbel-stone, about 2m above ground level, is an ancient marble block with visible inscriptions on two of its faces; just to its right is the base of an *anta* in the form of an inverted lion's claw which is also antique—other examples of which can be seen in the Archaeological Museum. Contemporary with this building, was the island's former 16th century cathedral church of **Aghios Vasílios Petrokókkinon**, whose floor and foundations are visible, sunk down below ground-level on the west side of the public gardens; the building was destroyed in 1822. The brick vaults of the crypt beneath, and the basilica floor-plan of the building, with three aisles and apses, can be clearly seen. The church's epithet (also the name of an important Chiot family), '*Petrokokkinon*' ('red rock'), comes from the deep red stone which is characteristic of the city's older buildings. Documents show that the church was rented by the catholic bishop of Chios for the purposes of celebrating the Latin rite—witness to the peaceful cohabitation of religious diversity in Chios in the 16th century. Close by these ruins, in the centre of the park, is the imposing **bronze statue** by the sculptor, Michalis Tombros (1889–1974) from Andros; it is his tribute to Constantine Kanaris, the admiral from the neighbouring island of Psará, who destroyed the flagship of the Ottoman navy in June 1822 in revenge for the Turkish massacres two months earlier. It is one of Tombros's most celebrated sculptures, and—though characteristically ponderous in feel—possesses a dramatic energy unusual for his works. Further east in Vounáki Square, the 19th century **marble fountain** is based on the Choragic Monument of Lysicrates below the acropolis in Athens.

Demokratia Street, which forms the northeastern boundary of the Gardens, is bordered by the *Demarchion* (Town Hall), and a row of *kafeneia* which have remained virtually unaltered since the 1950s—a measure of the innate conservatism and independence of the island's local culture. Half-way up Demokratia Street, where the road branches for Vrontados and the north of the island, is a free-standing marble **Ottoman fountain** bearing the (Hejira) date 1181, corresponding to 1763 in the western calendar. Although re-roofed, it conserves on all four sides its fine, original **carved decoration** in the florid style typical of the later Ottoman period. The fountain was built and donated by the Grand Vezir, Melik Pasha, who was of partly Chiot origin: the long inscriptions on the different faces are in praise of Chios, Chiots and the tradition of Greek history. The other Ottoman monument beside the park is the 19th century **Mecediye Mosque** to the southeast, which is currently undergoing restoration to re-house the island's **Byzantine Museum** (*open daily 8.30–1, except Mon*).

The courtyard and porch contain mostly salvaged items—Jewish and Muslim gravestones—and a number of interesting pieces of **Genoese Renaissance sculpture** from the 14th –16th centuries, as well as some Early Christian architectural elements. Particularly striking is the carved **sarcophagus** of Ottobuoni Giustiniani (1445) and the carved lintel-blocks, figuring the exploits of St George who was the patron saint of Genoa. In the interior is a display of the fine **18th century wall-paintings** executed by Michael Chomatzas, figuring scenes from the life of St Nicholas of Myra, which constituted the uppermost stratum of wall-painting in the church of the Panaghia Krina (near Vavíli, south of Chios—*see pp. 51–52*), removed and brought here in order to reveal lower, earlier strata of paintings still *in situ* in the church.

A smaller, but more noteworthy, Byzantine collection can be seen in the **Giustiniani 'Palace'** (*open daily 8.30–3, except Mon*) which lies 200m northeast from here along Kennedy St, just inside the main entrance gate of the Kastro. This contains some of the finest paintings on the island—detached once again from the walls of the church of the Panaghia Krina, but this time from the early 14th century layer in the cupola.

The twelve ***figures of *Saints* and *Prophets*** are of the very highest quality, and have survived with little damage (the lacunae at knee-height are the holes made for the fixing of the scaffolding when the cupola was later repainted): the monumentality and sculptural quality of *__Obadiah__* (no. 8), for example, is particularly striking and bears comparison with the almost contemporaneous works of Giotto in Italy: the latter are more tenaciously tactile and unstylised, yet without the dramatic elegance which these anonymous Byzantine works possess. Their quality would suggest a painter trained in Constantinople. Some allowance needs to be made to compensate for the fact that the viewer's position, when the figures were *in situ*, was from six metres below. (*Note: these paintings may eventually be transferred to the Byzantine Museum opposite the Public Garden, when renovations there are completed in late 2010.*) On the upper floor are also a number of fine 18th century, **icons** from Mestá and Olýmpi—amongst them, one of the **Archangel Michael**, cut and shaped around the outline of the saint for use in processions. This is an unusual genre of icon, found rarely outside of Chios.

The restored 16th century building which houses this collection, known as the 'Giustiniani Palace', was probably a guard-house or garrison headquarters for the castle. The large **guard-room** on the ground-floor (separate entrance through door just inside Main Gate, to right of stairs), is a beautiful example of brick vaulting supported on a central pier.

THE KASTRO

The **Fortress** or '**Kastro**' **of Chios**, which occupies a roughly rectangular area (c. 600m x 250m) to the north of the port, was surrounded by a moat filled with water and accessible only by means of a wooden drawbridge. The crescent shaped southeast wall which formed the northern boundary of the port and against whose wharfs the Genoese maritime fleet would have tied up, lies now a little way inland: it is the least well preserved section, by comparison with the north, east and west walls which stand intact and still possess their seven fine **bastions**. On this site there was no pre-existing stronghold: the Byzantine fortress appears to have stood some distance inland on higher ground. These fortifications are therefore principally Genoese, begun in the 1320s by the Zaccaria overlords and given new impetus in the early 1400s by the Giustiniani; only the northern bastion (the largest of all, and known as the '*Torrione Zeno*') was modified and enlarged by the Venetians in 1694/5 with more modern defensive technology, so as to include emplacements for their cannon—some fine examples of which can be seen in the courtyard of the city's Byzantine Museum opposite the Public Garden.

The **main gate**, or '*Porta Maggiore*', has been given a late 17th century outer facing by the Venetians during their brief stay, surmounted by a (partially erased) inscription recording Doge Silvestro Valier; behind it is the more functional 14th century Genoese gateway leading through the thickness of the walls. It is instructive to walk along the top of the enceinte, most of which is accessible, though divided by a breach for the street in the western corner. The northwestern sector is bisected by the massive 14th century **central bastion** bearing an eroded, triple **escutcheon** in marble of the Giustiniani family. To either side of the tower, on the inside of the walls, the clustered cupolas of two sets of **Ottoman baths** can be seen: these were in existence in the mid 18th century when Richard Chandler, Fellow of Magdalen College, Oxford, and member of the Dilettanti Society, sampled their pleasures on a visit to Chios in 1765; he later described the pummelling and contortions he received at the hands of the masseur of the *hamam*, whose 'feats … cannot easily be described, and are hardly credible'. The **sea-wall** of the castle is well-preserved and has remained unmodified from when it was built in the 14th century; its simple masonry and construction is of a different order of building from the meticulous and aristocratic structures of the Knights of St John on Kos and on Rhodes. Set-back to the south and a little inside, the round stack of the **Turkish watch-tower** rises above the level of the surrounding buildings.

The **interior of the Kastro**, which is still inhabited and lively, has preserved something of its former Levantine feel, with a number of the old lath-and-plaster house-fronts and projecting wooden balconies still to be seen along Aghios Giorgios Frouriou Street. This is the main axial street of the Kastro, running from the main gate to the church of Aghios Giorgios. At its southern end, inside the gate and to the west side, is the **Ottoman cemetery**, with most of its gravestones—inscribed and surmounted with a carved turban or fez—remaining well-preserved and intact. Amongst them (towards the back) it is a surprise to find the sarcophagus, decorated with flower-motif, of **Kara Ali Pasha**, the perpetrator of the Massacre of Chios of 1822. A little further north, set at an angle to all the other buildings is the four-square **Bayraklı Mosque**, dating from the late 18th century and now deprived of its porch and minaret; the spacious prayer-hall, surmounted by a shallow dome sitting on an interesting play of squinches, is in a state of abandon although the building has recently been re-roofed. Half-way down the length of the street, on the north side is the **church of Aghios Giorgios Frouriou**, whose orientation and proportions betray its origins also as a converted mosque. It sits in a courtyard which was once the *külliye* ('religious complex') of the mosque: on its northern side, under a plane-tree, is the former *sebil* or **fountain**—a fascinating assemblage of spolia which would originally have channelled the water pulled up from a well, into an ancient sarcophagus standing on two column-stumps and decorated with Ottoman designs in low relief, and thence into a stone washing-area for those preparing for prayer in the mosque.

NORTH OF THE KASTRO

Engravings and pictures of the city from the 16th to 18th centuries (in the Koraïs Library, *see below*) show the coast to the north of the city lined with **windmills**, a few of which remain today along the coast road. Nearly two kilometres north of the city on the road to Vrontados is a row of four restored mills on the edge of the sea: by turning left (west), two blocks inland from this point, you find the **church of Aghia Myrope and Aghios Isidoros** in a small square of the same name. Underneath the graceless concrete church are the substantial remains of the **Early Christian basilica** of the island's patron saint, St Isidore—a Roman legionary from Alexandria who was martyred in Chios in 251 AD, in the reign of Decius: the presence of his relics here must have made this the most important Early Christian site on the island—until 1125, that is, when his (headless) remains were stolen by the Venetians and later put in a marble sarcophagus in a chapel in St Mark's. The quantity of column fragments and **spolia** in fine Proconnesian marble outside, originally from pagan buildings, are testimony to the five successive Christian buildings that stood on this same site: the massive foundation blocks—rearranged from the crepidoma of an ancient temple—which delineate the form of the apse of the earliest basilica, are visible to the east. The treasure of the site is the large area of well-preserved, 5th–6th century *mosaic floor** in the interior. (*The key for the church is kept at no. 38, on the north side of the square, and hangs on the back side of the letter box.*) The abstract designs—knots, 'mill-sails', leaves and geometric shapes—are particularly fine and executed in only five colours of stone by someone who was clearly a master of the art. In view of the predominating 'windmill sail' motif in the field of the floor, it is interesting to note that there is a dedicatory inscription (now covered by the wooden floor) of '*Arkadeios, son of Phokaios, sailmaker*'. The crypt to the north side would have contained the tombs of the patronal saints.

The ancient '**Portasanta**' **marble-quarries** can also be visited in the area to the north of the town. (*Starting from the public gardens of Plateia Vounaki/Plastira, take the left diagonal branch after 100m—signed 'Theatro Latomeiou'—off the main road north to Vrontados; follow this for 2.2km; as the road descends, a ramp leads up left to the church of the Panaghia Latomítissa and to Aghios Nektarios; at the top of the hill, well above the church, are the main quarries.*) Given the widely varying qualities of this particular limestone, there are small quarrying assays all over the summit of the hill, easily recognisable by the curved, running striations left by the ancient cutting tools. The main quarry, in the form of a theatre-like declivity, is just below the summit. It was this stone—which varies from a mottled pink and white to a blue-grey with pink veins—that was probably used for constructing the walls of the ancient city. The marble takes its Renaissance name '*Portasanta*' from the fact that it was the stone used for the frame of the *Porta Santa*, or 'Holy Door', of St Peter's in Rome.

SOUTH OF THE CENTRE

Behind a sober pedimented façade on the south side of Korai Street, 500m south of the Main (Plastíra/Vounaki) Square, are the **Koraïs Library** and **Argentis Folklore Museum** (*open Mon–Fri 8–2*). The library, which was founded in the 18th century, is one of the most important in the Aegean. After the initial bequest of books in 1792 by the influential humanist and classical scholar from Smyrna, Adamantios Koraïs (1748–1833), the library has attracted the donation of many other collections—most recently the gift of an art and costume collection by Philip Argentis in 1948. The library and reading-rooms are downstairs and the Argentis Museum is on the upper floor. The collection is understandably long on family personalia and portraiture, but it contains nonethe-less some evocative and unusual pieces. The etchings and **drawings of houses in Kampos** are particularly revealing of the elegant lifestyle of their inhabitants; there are sev-eral sketches, copies and etchings relating to Delacroix's painting (1824) of the *Massacre of Chios*; a particularly fine watercolour of 1849, showing the deathbed scene of Marouko Argentis; a couple of perfectly executed 20th century miniatures on glass; carved wooden chests; and delicate **porcelain figurines** showing local costumes. One room is dedicated to the magnificent **collection of textiles**, which on Chios attain a particular beauty with their reds and pale green colours which are obtained from vegetable dyes. The city also has a small **Maritime Museum** (*open daily 10–2, except Sun*) at no. 20 Stefanou Tsouri Street (200m to the west of the Koraïs Library and the adjacent cathedral) which contains pictures, models and photographs of Aegean ships and maritime life, and memorabilia of Admiral Kanaris. It is housed in a grand, early 20th century mansion of the Pateras family—one of the most important shipping families of Oinousses and Chios.

ARCHAEOLOGICAL MUSEUM

Two blocks in from the south west corner of the harbour, are the buildings of the **University of the Aegean** which stand behind an attractive garden of palms; next to them is the island's *****Archaeological Museum**, between Mouseiou and Michalon Streets, which should not be missed. (*Open daily 8.30–3, except Mon.*) Both the richness and the idiosyncracy of Chios have been mentioned above in the general context of the island's character: in the collection of antiquities from the island, these qualities emerge as primary once again in the remarkable variety and unusualness of some of the categories of objects—in particular, the rare and moving grave *stelai* with fluid, incised designs from the Hellenistic period which are almost unique to Chios. The collection is laid out on three levels in a custom-designed building of 1970, with six principal rooms or zones.

Room I (to right of entrance): exhibits prehistoric finds (Neolithic through to Bronze Age) principally from the cave at Aghio Gala in the northwest of the island and from the excavations at Emporeio in the south. The same categories of object recur—jugs, cups, *pyxes*—but in a wide variety of forms and designs, occasionally with incised decoration. One fragment of the lid of a receptacle (*no. 104*) is carved in the form of a dog's head. With the Mycenaean Age (*central display-case*), simple, bold **decorative designs** of great beauty begin to arrive. The Protogeometric (9th century BC) vases from excavations in the city of Chios show clear influences from Euboea and the Northern Cyclades, confirming the direction of settlement in this crucial period.

Room II (subdivided): contains the wide variety of objects in stone from historic times, beginning with two striking ***torso fragments of korai**, of the early 6th century (580–570) BC. What is unusual here are the lightly incised, undulating **folds of the chitons** they wear, beautifully conceived on the shoulders and back in particular, as well as the position of the hands beneath the falling locks of hair (*no. 225*): at this early stage a quite distinct and naturally graceful Ionic style is developing. *Kore no. 226* once held an appliqué offering to her bosom. In the case along the wall is a wide selection of votive offerings, ornaments and modelled figurines—beginning with the earliest representational piece to have been found on the island, a **Late Neolithic male head** from Aghio Gala. One late 7th century BC find from Emporeio is the well-preserved **head of a helmeted warrior** (*no. 2, right show-case*) with remarkably fine **painted detail**, once the top of an *aryballos* (a perfume or oil container). In the corner of the room is a display of images of the seated Mother-goddess, **Cybele**, found in a remarkably wide distribution of sites on the island; it shows the importance of the cult of the divinity (Anatolian in origin) on Chios and helps to make sense of the site of the sanctuary of Cybele at Vrontados, commonly known also as 'Homer's Seat' (*see below*).

Behind the central, dividing display-case is the collection of exquisitely *incised limestone grave *stelai* of the 5th to 3rd centuries BC—a type of *stele* which is virtually exclusive to Chios, depicting seated figures, dancing girls or birds in flight, sketched with a delicacy sometimes more fluid even than ancient vase-painting. Especially clear are *no. 665* (5th century BC) with images of waterfowl and *no. 280* (3rd century BC) with a seated **lyre-player**. The end of the hall exhibits some well-conserved **Roman portrait busts**, including a rare and sensitive **portrait of Sabina** (*no. 5636*), wife of the Emperor Hadrian. Underscoring the importance of Dionysos for a wine-producing island such as Chios is a display of figures and heads of the god from different periods.

Room III (parallel to, and integral with, the previous gallery): continues the theme of wine-trading, with a collection of **Chiot *amphorae***, displayed so as to show their chronological development: from the heavier, swollen-neck designs of the 6th century BC, through the 5th century

Siren playing a Lute.
Incised image on a limestone grave *stele* from Chios, 3rd century BC.
(Archaeological Museum of Chios)

BC cylindrical-neck design, to the later Hellenistic forms with narrow bodies and long necks, modified for more efficient storage in the holds of boats. There is also an official **liquid-measure standard** in marble. The rest of the room is devoted to **inscriptions**— fascinating for what they tell us about the workings of a community, its legislation, voting, and—clearly shown here—the frequent cooperation in judicial matters and in arbitration between one island and another. Most important amongst this collection are two ***engraved epistles from Alexander the Great to the Chiots** (who had previously sided with Athens against Macedon)—the first (*no. 39*), inscribed in 332 BC, restoring a democratic regime to the island and ordering the return of political exiles; the second (*no. 68*) requesting clemency for an acquaintance who was on trial as a pro-Persian traitor. The far end of the room exhibits a collection of **grave *stelai*** of the more usual type found across the Hellenic world: nearly all are scenes of banquets for the dead, mourning widows or valedictions: a notable exception is *no. 10189* (2nd century BC) which depicts a solitary, dignified **male figure**, standing with his hands crossed before him.

Room IV (mezzanine): houses principally the museum's collection of vases, metalwork and jewellery, with the addition of one case exhibiting a 2nd century BC human skull which shows interesting evidence of **surgical trepanning**. The displays of vases have good didactic material explaining the progressive development of local ceramic work: there is a fine collection of fragments of the so-called, 6th century BC '**wild-goat style**' (witness the confident depiction of these animals on *no. 15, no. 16 & no. 18*); a new manganese-red colour is introduced in *no. 21 & no. 22*. The central show-case has a rich display of bronze and ivory work, and includes a couple of the museum's most unusual treasures—a carved *****ivory horse and rider** of the 7th century BC, no larger than a walnut, with beautifully executed hands holding the bridle; and a minuscule (4cm), late 6th century BC, **gilded silver figurine of a hel-** **meted warrior** (*no. 10*) from the sanctuary of Apollo at *Phanai*. The collection of Hellenistic **gold fillets**, wreaths and decorations, include some **pendants** of striking intricacy: one (*no. 104*) is of a female figure riding a panther. The island's coins—with their characteristic Sphinx (obverse) and *amphora* (reverse), are represented here mostly in casts: the originals are in museums and collections elsewhere.

Room V displays a number of remarkable architectural elements which illustrate well the latent tendency towards animism always present in Ionian architecture: the colossal, **sculpted, four-toed lion's paws**, from Emporeio, are in fact *antae* **bases**, i.e. the bases of flush pilasters against the front wall of the *naos* in the entrance porch of a temple. They are marginally later (5th century BC) than the fragments of **ionic capitals**, and **sections of friezes** and entablatures from the 6th century BC temple of Apollo at *Phanai*, but they share the same bold design and stylistic vigour.

Room VI (on the upper floor) is dedicated solely to finds from the neighbouring island of **Psará**, most of which come from excavations of **Mycenaean graves** at Archontikí on the island's west coast (*see pp. 160–161*). There is an impressive quantity of pottery (including graceful, stemmed *kylixes*, and stirrup-jars with decoration), gold artefacts, bronze swords (which are helpful in dating the burials) and jewellery, all from between the 14th and 12th centuries BC. The gentle, natural colours and subtlety of the **gemstone jewellery** and **necklaces in faience and glass-paste**, are particularly striking.

Outside courtyard: the largest exhibit in the open area behind the museum is the reassembled, 2nd century BC **Macedonian-style mausoleum**—constructed from perfectly cut ashlar, stone blocks of different colours—found in 1980 in the outskirts of Chios town. The delicate crown of oak-leaves, fashioned in beaten gold, on display in Room IV, was part of the grave-goods found in its interior chamber. The courtyard contains more fine architectural fragments and elements—amongst them, an exquisitely **carved pilaster capital** (early 5th century BC), with three interlocking and **superimposed scrolls**, with palmette and rosette decorations. The design is similar to surviving elements from the Great Altar of Hera on Samos, though the decoration is more intricate, as would be expected in a piece created almost a hundred years later.

THE KAMPOS

Everything that may disappoint in the architecture of Chios town today, is compensated for by the unique beauty of the **Kampos* area. Although a shadow of what it once was before the massacres of 1822, the earthquake of 1881 and the encroachment of the airport and city periphery, the area's patrician villas and churches, wooded gardens, and the warmth of the variegated red stone from which everything is built, still combine to make this one of the most atmospheric and architecturally significant suburbs in the Greek world. The area lies 4–5km due south of Chios, in the plain bounded by the city to the north, the shoreline to the east, and the village of Thymianá to the south. It is reached either by cutting inland from the coast after the south end of the airport runway, or by following signs for 'Neochóri' and 'Thymianá' from the centre of town: it is a labyrinth of high-walled streets and water-channels which can only really be explored serendipitously. It would be cumbersome to describe a particular itinerary here; only general observations, therefore, to help the visitor understand its genesis and character are offered below.

History and development

The eastern sides and slopes of island mountain-ranges benefit from ideal conditions for fruit-growing; softer water, greater rainfall and humidity, cool moisture early in the day's cycle and remission from the dry air and winds that areas facing the sunset receive. For these reasons, the Kampos area was the main cultivated area for the city of Chios from Antiquity onwards. In the 14th and 15th centuries the Genoese masters of the island built towers, or *pyrgi*, in this area: these were not watch-towers, but rather glorified tool-sheds and residences for farm-managers, built sturdily so as to mark and protect their estates. In the greater security afforded by Ottoman occupation, these *pyrgi* gradually were turned into **summer retreats** on **family estates**, becoming eventually necessary status symbols for any family of substance. The important merchant families, who had a combination of wealth to dispose from trading in the island's produce and experience, through their travels, of the great city suburbs in Egypt, Italy and the Levant coast, began to compete in the construction of ever finer villas and residences, adopting some of the architectural lessons learnt from overseas. They also built '**family' churches** in the area as a further expression of status—always using the same tender red stone. The late 18th and early 19th century was the short-lived heyday of this area: not long after, the majority of the owners were rounded up and exemplarily killed in the 1822 massacre, and many of the houses were abandoned or suffered subsequent destruction in the earthquake of 1881, which was of a magnitude of 6.5 on the Richter scale. For these reasons only a few of the villas remain—some maintained as before, some restored (more or less faithfully), and others in a state of ruin.

The design of the villas

The villas functioned both as farmhouses for the family estate, and as country residences: hence they are surrounded by low storage buildings and **stone barns**, and centred on a shaded courtyard around the **well** from which the water was drawn by a yoked donkey treading in a circle. The sound of creaking wooden machinery and splashing water would have lasted throughout the day. In this manner the *sterna*— a deep stone cistern, often covered with a pergola supported on pillars at the corners—was filled with water, which was then channelled throughout the estate to irrigate the citrus and fruit trees, whose colour aptly set off the deep red of the stone used in the high walls which invariably surrounded them. The sleeping and reception rooms were on the upper floors of the buildings, illuminated with long windows and giving onto **shaded terraces and balconies**, from which it was possible to see—and be seen—above the walls. Access to this upper area is generally by a grand **stone staircase** on the outside of the building, whose landings and balustrades are punctuated with carved **stone urns**. The overall design is prevailingly Italian—distantly reminiscent of suburban villas in Genoa—but the decorative gateways onto the street often have an Ottoman flavour in their alternating use of two colours of stone in the arches, and the porch-like roofs which cover them.

The protected micro-climate of Chios town is particularly well-suited to the cultivation of citrus fruits, and many of the walled gardens of Kampos are still given over to orchards of lemon, orange, mandarin and other fruit trees. The scent, when the tress are in flower, overwhelms the air. An informative, permanent exhibition, entitled '*Citrus*', recounting the cultivation of the trees and the preparation of a variety of citrus products has been created in the fine villa at nos 9–11 Argentis Street in Kampos—home also of the *Perivoli Hotel* (*see lodging, p. 134*).

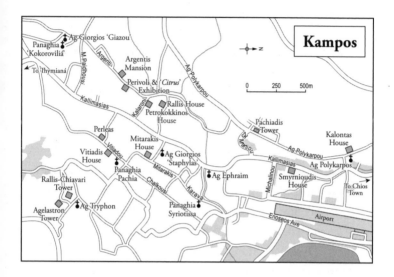

Both the main arterial street from Chios to Neochóri through the centre of Kampos, and the parallel streets (e.g. Argenti Street, to the west) pass many monumental entrances, behind which hide groves of flowering trees and the façades of houses. The textures and colours—of cypress and pine trees, of red and ochre-coloured walls—combined with the smells of citrus flower and the sounds of birds and occasional running water, give a fleeting sense of the tranquillity, elegance and beauty of this area which was so repeatedly commented on by visitors from overseas in past centuries. A number of the churches in the area—many with unusual epithets—are signposted:

Aghios Giorgios 'Ghiázou', Panaghia 'Kokoroviliá', Pan-aghia 'Syriótissa' etc. All date from the 19th century and most were restored after the earthquake of 1881: the exteriors have nothing Byzantine in their design and are prevailingly western in form, but the lavish—often baroque—decoration of the interiors, with an ostentatious display of gold leaf, is nonetheless of Orthodox layout. What unites all the architectural elements of this area is the distinctive 'poros' stone, richly coloured by the presence of iron oxides. The **quarries**—ancient in origin and still in use today—which lie in the hills between **Thymianá** and Karfás, produce a stone which varies in colour from an ochre orange, through all shades of pinks and reds, to a deep magenta, depending on exactly where in the quarry the stone is cut.

THE YPAPANTI CHAPEL &
JULIETTE MAY FRASER

In the village of **Vavíli** (7.5km from Chios) at the southwestern corner of the Kampos plain is one of the island's most unexpected treasures—the minuscule **chapel of the Ypapanti** (the 'Purification of the Virgin'), whose interior is entirely covered with *murals, painted in 1963 by Ju-

liette May Fraser (1887–1983), an artist from Honolulu.
(*The chapel is c. 200m north of the main village church of
Aghios Nikolaos, on 'Odos May Fraser'. Key kept in house
opposite and slightly further north.*)

The majority of Juliette May Fraser's work has remained
in the Hawaiian islands where she was born and died, and
where she was commissioned to decorate the State Library.
While working in Athens in the early 1960s she volunteered
to paint these murals, together with the artist David Asher-
man, as a gift to the village. The outside of the chapel is
decorated with geometrical patterns in *sgraffito* (partly coloured), recalling the distinctive exteriors of the houses in
Pyrgí. The interior is fresh in colour and clear in design. Not
unexpectedly, the scenes are a hybrid of eastern and western, Byzantine and representational, modern and ancient;
the perspective comes and goes; the scenes are sometimes
(such as the *Presentation* itself) in local topography, sometimes in eternal landscapes; a musician angel plays an ac-
cordion, another has Hawaiian physiogmony. The whole is
unified by an airiness and overall brilliance of colour, and is
executed with such genuine joy that it provides a valuable
counterpoint to the island's wealth of early Byzantine art—
one of the best examples of which, the Panaghia Krína, is to
be found nearby in the foothills, 2.5km west of Vavíli.

THE PANAGHIA KRINA

(The church, currently finishing a long restoration-programme is in a solitary location, signposted, mid-way between Sklaviá and Vavíli.)

Sophisticated in design and beautifully decorated with blind arches and lively **brick patterns** on the exterior and with paintings inside, this is a church close in date and in architectural conception to *Nea Moni*. It appears to have been a 12th century Constantinopolitan commission, donated by two members of the Imperial Court, Eustathius Codratos and Irene Doucaina Pagomene—though both the reason for its commission and the remote setting remain unclear. The presence of pagan and Early Christian **spolia** in the outer belfry-wall, the threshold, and beside the entrance of the narthex (column bases, fragments of cornice and a frieze with **garlanded *bucrania*** etc.), suggests preceding buildings, going perhaps as far back as a pagan shrine, on this spot. From outside, the similarities to *Nea Moni* are clear: the **dynamic profile**—a steep drum and cupola over the sanctuary with another, smaller dome over the narthex; the materials and brick patterns (especially the **decorated lunette** over the narthex entrance); and the long linear axis preceding the *naos*, through an exonarthex (18th century) and a transverse narthex (12th century). Once inside, the dignified and luminous **octagonal** *naos* is even more redolent of *Nea Moni*.

It is from this church that the two series of wall paintings exhibited in Chios (the 14th century paintings from the cupola, in Palazzo Giustiniani, and the upper layer of 18th century paintings from the naos, in the Byzantine Museum: *see pp. 27–29*) have been removed so as to reveal the original **12th century paintings** which now decorate the main area and which are of a quality which suggests the hand of an artist from Constantinople. Some small areas of the upper layer of 18th century paintings by Michael Chomatzas (1734) are preserved—of particular note, the **allegorical scene** to the left of the passage between the narthex and the *naos*, depicting an extravagantly dressed merchant holding a naked, allegorical figure by the hair, whose clearly urgent meaning remains nonetheless obscure.

A little more than a kilometre south from Panaghia Krina, towards **Sklaviá**, standing to the east of the road in the midst of a landscape densely covered with olive, mulberry and cypress, is a large corbelled **Genoese** *pyrgos* dating from the 15th/16th century. This is a good example of the kind of building, mentioned above, which formed the nucleus of the private estates of the Kampos area and which were often replaced by, or incorporated into, the later villas that survive in greater numbers today.

CENTRAL CHIOS & *NEA MONI*

The main road due west from Chios town rises steadily, passing (1.3km) the modern monastery of the Panaghia Voitheía (the 'Virgin of Succour') (*right side*), built at the site of an abundant freshwater **spring** (*left side*) whose mineral waters are still popular with locals who come here to collect them. There are more springs in the village of **Karyés**, which is built on a 'shelf' below the escarpments of Mount Troúlos, and is reached by a detour from the road at 3.2km from Chios. From the ridge of the cliff-like escarpment north and west of Karyés, was extracted in Antiquity one of the loveliest of all ancient polychrome marbles, known today by the post-Renaissance name of **Breccia di Aleppo**. The marble is characterised by a pale grey and brick-coloured ground, scattered with prominent, golden-yellow *breccie*. It has nothing to do with Aleppo (an error in taxonomy caused by the mistranscription of the name of a quarry of similar stone in Southern France), but in fact comes from this small quarry on Chios, which to this day shows signs of ancient cutting and is littered with potsherds of the Hellenistic and Roman period.

After 6km the road climbs steeply in switchbacks, with magnificent **views** opening into the Turkish mainland: the hillside is dotted with other monasteries, churches and hermitages, all of which profited from the spiritual and clerical traffic that the presence of *Nea Moni* attracted. One of these (*left turn at 8.8km*) is the intimate **monastery of Aghios Markos**. Hosios Parthenios, who was the principal force behind the rebuilding of *Nea Moni* after the earthquake of 1881, is buried here: his hermitic cave-cell is on the hill below (*obtain key from monastery*) beside a stand of fir-trees, with serene views to the sea below.

NEA MONI AND AGHII PATERAS

A little more than half a kilometre further along the principal road is a left turn for **Nea Moni* (3km) which, for its mosaics and architectural design, is one of most significant Byzantine churches of the Greek world. (*Currently undergoing far-reaching restoration (2009). Normally open daily 8—1, 4–7. Appropriate dress required.*) From the approaching road, the beauty of the **setting** is immediately visible—amongst ancient trees in a verdant fold of the mountains, superbly hidden yet panoramic, solitary yet surrounded by a cluster of ruined buildings that huddle under the general mantle of its protection. In an illustration from the *Travels of Basil Grigorovich Barsky in the Holy Places of the East, from 1723 to 1747* (in the Koraïs Library) the monastery is pictured as a small city teeming with buildings and people; prominent in the depiction are the enceinte of walls, and the **fortified guard-tower** at the western extremity. Today the out-buildings are mostly abandoned shells; the **arcaded aqueduct** no longer brings water from the north into the magnificent, **11th century cisterns**. The monastery never recovered fully from the two catastrophes of the 19th century—the Turkish destruction of 1822 which was visited with particular severity on those who sought to take refuge here, and the earthquake almost 60 years later in 1881. The **chapel of the Holy Cross**, immediately to the left of the gate on entering, functions as an **ossuary** and memorial to those killed here in 1822. The main *catholicon* sits in the open space at the heart of the buildings, just ahead.

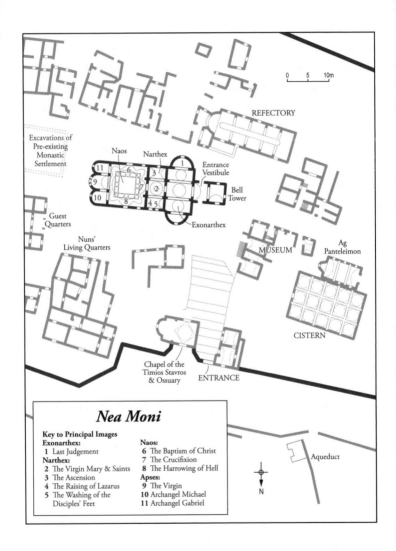

REFECTORY

Excavations of
Pre-existing
Monastic
Settlement

Naos   Narthex

Entrance
Vestibule

Bell
Tower

Exonarthex

Guest
Quarters

Nuns'
Living Quarters

MUSEUM

Ag
Panteleimon

CISTERN

Chapel of the
Timios Stavros
& Ossuary   ENTRANCE

Aqueduct

N

Nea Moni

Key to Principal Images
Exonarthex:
  1 Last Judgement
Narthex:
  2 The Virgin Mary & Saints
  3 The Ascension
  4 The Raising of Lazarus
  5 The Washing of the
    Disciples' Feet

Naos:
  6 The Baptism of Christ
  7 The Crucifixion
  8 The Harrowing of Hell
Apses:
  9 The Virgin
  10 Archangel Michael
  11 Archangel Gabriel

The foundation

The **name** is curious: the monastery is in fact dedicated to the Dormition of the Virgin in commemoration of the finding of a miraculous icon of the Virgin on the mountainside in the early 11th century; but it has been universally known as '*Nea Moni*', or the 'New Monastery', ever since it received its endowment from the Emperor of Byzantium in 1042 and was renewed as a grander complex at the site of a pre-existing hermitage, founded by three hermits. The remains of this marginally **earlier monastery** are being uncovered by excavations a few metres further to the east of the present *catholicon*. The Imperial gifts of money, land and materials, as well as the providing of the architects and artesans who constructed the '*Nea Moni*', were the fulfillment of a vow made by Constantine IX Monomachos, when the three hermits living on this site predicted his return from exile in Lesbos to Constantinople to become Emperor. His consort, and co-founder, was the remarkable Empress Zoë, through whom the line of Imperial succession passed—a virgin apparently until she was 50 years old, after which age she enjoyed three nuptials to successive ruling Emperors, the last of which was to Constantine. Their portraits may still be seen in one of the few mosaics to have survived in the Gallery of Santa Sophia in Istanbul. Building and decoration were both largely completed by 1056.

The architecture

Great Byzantine painting of the 11th century is profoundly stylised—and the architecture of this building, no less so. Viewed both from the east or from the side, the width and height of the megalocephalic drum and cupola of the *catholicon* dominate the profile of the building inordinately. There are highly 'stylised' proportions also in the floor-plan of the church: for example, the narrow transverse exonarthex is wider than any other part of the church; and the four-square plan of the *naos* evolves into eight, unequal conches as it rises, which subsequently dissolve into the circle of the dome, by an architectural sleight of hand.

This is not stylisation for the sake of stylisation: it is part of a conscious intention on the part of the architects to give spiritual meaning to the progression of the worshipper through the spaces of the church—from the narrow, dark areas of the narthex and exonarthex, to the magnificently luminous, high space of the *naos*. It is this that creates the dramatic effects of the interior. This is further enhanced in the *naos* by the complex vertical passage from square plan to circular cupola, through an octagonal intermediary; this has the practical effect of leaving the central space free of supporting piers, as well as giving a rhythm of alternating narrow and wide conches or niches. In all these ways, *Nea Moni* (1042) contrasts interestingly with its near contemporary, the Monastery of St John on Patmos (1088): the church of the latter is a humble structure, modestly decorated with painting, and completely un-ambitious in design; here, at *Nea Moni*, costly mosaics and the full power of architectural sophistication and innovation from the Imperial capital have been brought to bear.

The exterior

In addition to the intriguing and complex grouping of roofs and cupolas in the profile of the *catholicon*, the material from which the building is made, and the decorative effects to which it is put, are unusual. Brick is not generally a common material in the Greek Islands, even though on Chios there are several notable examples of its use in ecclesiastical buildings. There is no evidence of brick kilns near to *Nea Moni*, and the material must have been transported laboriously from the area of Chalkeio or from Kambos, far below. The walls are composed of mixed stone and brick-tiles. The tiles are used extensively for the work of defining arches, framing windows, and forming a varying entablature of decoration; they erupt exuberantly in places as a sunburst design (north side) or as a heart (south side) between two blind arches—apparently for the sheer joy of decoration.

Elevation of the *catholicon* of *Nea Moni* (1056), looking east from the entrance vestibule, showing the highly stylised proportion of the cupola to the lower body of the church.

The interior

The interior is a dramatic procession of spaces of different forms, heights, colours and kinds of decoration: a rectangular atrium next to the belfry, which is entered first, precedes an exonarthex, which precedes a narthex, which precedes the *naos*—each stage more finely decorated than the previous. Such a succession of spaces at Santa Sophia in Constantinople was linked to the demands of processional ceremony—related principally to the entry of the Emperor into the building, who symbolically transformed himself from temporal to religious monarch as he progressed from one vestibule to the next: here at *Nea Moni*, however, the complexity of design is more an expression of the Imperial interest that lay behind the building's creation. The **atrium** or vestibule is floored with plain slabs and fragments of ancient marble, and the posts of the doorway between the atrium and the exonarthex are of Chios's native portasanta marble (from Latomi, north of Chora) surmounted by grey limestone capitals. In the next area—the **exonarthex**—the floor is magnificently inlaid with polychrome marbles in a design of five interlocked rings. The space has apses both to north and south, making it the widest element of the complex. It was decorated with paintings on plaster of which only fragments now remain: best preserved is the complex figuration of the *Last Judgement* in the south apse. As a kind of decoration, wall-painting was considered very much a 'second-best' alternative to the much more costly work in mosaic: here it functions as a kind of 'appetiser' for the mosaics which follow.

The display of *mosaics begins in the yet darker and more confined space of the **narthex**: in this area their designs were set off by the low, flickering light of candles and lamps, rather than by steady daylight. Together with those at Hosios Loukas (near Delphi) and Dafni (near Athens), the cycle here and in the *naos*—though fragmentary—is one of the three most important still surviving in Greece. The mosaics are of the highest quality technically and stylistically, and are closely related to those (the Imperial portraits, mentioned above) in the Gallery of Santa Sophia in Constantinople—if not actually by the same workshop of artists. They are contemporaneous with the construction of the building itself between 1042 and 1056. The balance of empty space and design, the clarity of the figures and the dignified richness of the colour, make them works of Byzantine Art of the highest order, wholly at one with the architecture of their setting. Nothing is superfluous to their illustrative purpose; nowhere are the scenes overcrowded.

They are executed in a combination of different materials: *tesserae* of both coloured stone and glass-paste create the colours of the figurative and decorative designs, and *tesserae* made in the ancient technique of fusing gold-leaf in clear glass form the glittering, celestial background. The colours are particularly delicate and subdued; the prevailing muted-greens and browns are always contrasted and set off in each image by small elements of a rich red colour—the figure in a red robe to the side of the magnificent *Baptism of Christ*, or the red slippers of the Virgin Mary as she stands beside the solemn *Crucifixion*. The ample and spacious gold backgrounds unify the whole cycle. Gold is used here, as it is in the backgrounds of icons, as a symbol of the unchanging and eternal context in which these scenes are placed, because gold, too is unchanging and eternal—never forming compounds, never oxidising or rusting as the baser metals do. The scenes are to be read as icons of eternal truths, rather than naturalistic depictions of scenes set against a worldly background.

The images of the ceiling of the narthex are principally of *Saints, Martyrs* and *Prophets* grouped protectively around the central presence of the *Virgin* in the cupola (now damaged), with the beautifully conceived figures in the pendentives below of her parents, *Joachim* and *Anna*, and of *Saints Panteleimon* and *Stephen*. On the eastern wall are figurative scenes of the *Raising of Lazarus*, and of the *Ascension*, witnessed by a magnificent group of robed spectators; on the north wall is the *Washing of the Disciples' Feet*—an in-

genious polyphony of different gestures of dismay and reti-
cence.

The culmination of the architectural progression of mod-
ulating spaces comes as you are 'released' from the cramped
darkness of the *narthex* and emerge into the resplendent
space and luminousness of the **naos**. The architecture de-
fines a space that is no longer earthbound and enclosed, but
vertical in thrust and uplifting in feel, towards the crown-
like cupola which is pierced with tall windows letting in the
light from above. Today the light passes through clear glass.
In the 11th century the windows were perhaps of translu-
cent alabaster or a golden coloured glass—giving a quite different and warmer quality of light. The technology for the
creation of clear glass was only mastered several centuries
later in Venice.

The decorative plan of the *naos* is far more wide-rang-
ing, and is seen in a space whose light is wholly different.
The *Pantocrator* and *Angels* of the cupola were lost in the
earthquake of 1881, but the important scenes in the conches
have mostly survived—the *Baptism* (south), the *Crucifixion*
(west), and the *Harrowing of Hell* (north). These are the finest scenes of all—each balanced, in similar pattern, around
the central, axial figure of Christ. In the *Crucifixion*, the solitary and tragic dignity of Mary and St John to either side, is
delicately underscored by the presence of the two women

and the Roman centurion, placed to the side of each respectively. The culminating image of the *Virgin* in the central apse behind the *templon* has only survived in the lower portions, flanked by the *Archangels Michael* and *Gabriel* in the two lateral apse conches. The weightless shimmer of the mosaics overhead, especially when illuminated in the dark, is balanced by the **coloured marbles** underfoot and around the walls: the polished, dark-red glow of the local poros stone, relieved with variegated *portasanta*, predominates and links the interior colour to the overall red hue of the brick exterior. Some areas, where the original marble revetment has been lost (especially in the west wall of the *naos*), have been painted with *faux marbre* instead. In the north wall of the sanctuary behind the templon is a small carved holy **water-stoup** inside the *prothesis* niche.

Of the surrounding monastery buildings, many of those which originally housed the cells of the monastic community are now in ruins. The original **refectory** (restored and re-roofed) survives to the southwest of the catholicon; it is a long, luminous hall, with an apse to the east, down the central axis of which runs the original **11th century stone refectory-table** inlaid with large designs in **polychrome marbles**. A cobbled street to the west leads past the chapel of St Panteleimon (1889) towards the ruined, four-square **tower** at the western extremity of the enceinte which used to house the library. The books and the treasury of the monastery mostly disappeared when the monastery was torched during the 1822 massacres; for this reason the small **museum**, on the upper floor of the building across the courtyard to the northwest of the bell-tower, contains a limited collection of largely 19th century liturgical items and icons, except for some fine, embroidered 18th century pieces—amongst them a fine *epigonation* with a depiction of the *Last Supper,* and a girdle with intricately carved, silver buckle.

Behind the museum building and slightly to the northwest is an arch elaborately framed with tiles which gives onto the magnificent 11th century **cistern building**, whose deep rectangular form is roofed with 15 vaults supported on marble columns. Once again, its design is Constantinopolitan—a recollection of the elaborate and spacious cisterns of the capital city.

Today only one frail and elderly nun, followed in her peregrinations around the buildings by a flock of chickens, doves and cats, still inhabits *Nea Moni.* Costly and far-reaching restoration-works are underway in the complex, involving the re-pointing of the brick-work with modern mortar, and the renewing of the window-frames and templon screen with machine-cut marble. The new

generation of monks or nuns—if there should be one—
will inherit a church whose once crepuscular interior,
darkened with smoke and animated by the sounds of gut-
tering candles and a ticking grandfather clock, will now
be crisp and clean as never before.

The nearby **monastery of the Aghii Pateras**, built in
the late 19th century on a scale that dwarfs the size of *Nea
Moni*, lies higher up the mountain and a little less than
a kilometre to the west. (*Reached by a path directly from
Nea Moni, or by road—returning to the island's main east/
west road (3.3km) from Nea Moni, continuing 1.2km west,
and taking a panoramic road left (1.6km) for the monastery.*) The large complex of buildings—now home to four
monks—has grown up around a **hermit's cave**, which
was first closed by a church (lower level) in the 17th century. The main *catholicon*, on the upper level, has unusual
wall-paintings of the 1890s that cover all the wall space
of its chancel, showing the massed ranks of the Holy Fa-
thers, to whom the church is dedicated.

AVGONYMA AND ANAVATOS

One kilometre after the turning for Aghii Pateras, the
main road reaches the watershed and begins to descend
the western slopes of the island through a wild area,
densely treed with pine. The first habitation is encoun-
tered at **Avgónyma** (16km from Chios) which crowns
the spur of a hill with wide views out to sea and prof-
its from a shallow and fertile plateau for cultivation. The
cuboid houses of varying hue and dimensions give the
village the appearance of a study by Cézanne. There was
a settlement here in Antiquity; today the village, grouped
around an open stone-paved square, shows its Genoese
origins of the 15th century in the features of its houses—
window-frames, machicolations, buttresses, and general
style of masonry. It is a fine architectural ensemble; but
it is outshone in setting and atmosphere, by its remarkable neighbour, ***Anávatos**—one of the most dramatically sited villages in the Aegean and, like Olympos on
Karpathos, one of the most isolated up until the recent
advent of asphalt roads. The 4km detour to the north of
the main road from Avgónyma is of great beauty, wind-
ing through mature pine forest and clearings which are
rich in wild flowers. Only at the very last moment is the
visitor confronted by a vision of the magnificent and in-

accessible site of the village, occupying the north face of a limestone precipice, whose south and west sides plummet almost vertically into a gorge.

The name 'Anávatos' is cognate with the Greek verb '*ἀναβαίνειν*', 'to climb' or 'scale'. The natural acropolis of the summit has a number of advantages which may explain its improbable choice as a place of settlement: apart from formidable natural defences, a deep, sinuous gorge to the west gave direct and quick access to the bay of Elinda which cuts into the central part of the west coast—the stretch most heavily fortified by the Genoese with watch-towers for protection against piracy. Anávatos and Avgónyma are also the closest points to Chios town that survey the western approaches to the island; they were vital links therefore in the defence of the island as a whole. An unverifiable local tradition holds that Anávatos was founded by the wood-cutters and timber-men brought to Chios to make scaffolding for the construction of *Nea Moni*, implying settlement as early as the 11th century; it must then later have been further fortified to form part of the Genoese system of defences. It appears to have been a flourishing community at the time of the massacres of 1822 which abruptly terminated its existence and gave rise to the abandonment of the site. The inhabitants, spurred by a combination of desperation and pride, are said to have thrown themselves over the western cliff rather than yield to capture by their Turkish assailants. It is a measure of the implacable fury of the Turks that they should have pursued their punitive cause so deep into the interior of the island. A shadow still hangs over the village.

The tiers of uninhabited houses, built in un-rendered stone, are perfectly camouflaged against the limestone escarpments; they have the form of towers, with the minimum necessary perforations for windows, which are only rarely embellished with a small relieving arch above the frame. The stepped streets lead up to the **fortress** at the summit, where a curtain wall—part constructed, part natural—encloses an area dominated by the ruins of a **double-nave church** (with vestiges of late painting in the apse). This design of such a building with two parallel naves, can often arise from the contemporaneous need for the celebration of both the Latin and Orthodox rites, suggesting a latterly mixed community here of Genoese and local Greeks.

THE CENTRAL WEST COAST

The road from Chios via Avgónyma meets the west coast road at 23km. This wild and dramatic coastline is regularly punctuated by cylindrical, mediaeval **Genoese watchtowers**, placed strategically on successive rises or promontories. The network gives a sense of the thoroughness and tenacity with which the the Genoese defended this rich outpost of their trading empire. (*See box below, pp. 100–102.*) The towers above the bays of **Tigáni** (9km north) and **Trachíli** (2.5km south) are well conserved and easily accessible. Another marks the entrance to the **bay of Elinda**, immediately north of the road junction. This protected and beautiful inlet of turquoise water, with a pebble strand, was the 'harbour' for Anávatos and Avgónyma: occasionally its colour is distilled for a fleeting moment in a glimpse of the kingfishers which sometimes frequent the bay.

Twelve kilometres to the north is the village of **Sideroúnta**, which straggles along an eminence above the west coast. A track to the west, just 50m beyond the turning into the village, descends steeply to the sea below (1.3km), where a spring of slightly alkaline water rises just above the shoreline. In the base of the valley formed by the seasonal torrents, 200m inland to the north, is the church of **Aghios Ioannis**, which still preserves late Byzantine (17th/18th century) **paintings** in its east end. The faces of *SS John Chrysostom and Basil* below the figure of Christ in the apse, are finely painted and well-preserved; the scenes of the *Passion* in the vault have survived less well. A further 2km north along the coastal track is the isolated church of **Aghios Giorgios Prastias**, on a rise to the east: here the paintings, which cover the whole of the interior, are substantially older (mostly 15th century), but in poorer condition—blackened, and in danger of detaching. The church was built in 1415 by Battista Giustiniani: but the reasons for a Genoese overlord to build a small, orthodox chapel in such a remote rural area remain unclear. The presence of a few well-cut and drafted blocks of limestone scattered around the area of both of these churches—with some blocks incorporated in the construction of the buildings—suggests a presence along the coast here which goes as far back as classical antiquity.

North of Siderounta (at 17km from the junction with the road from Avgónyma) the west coast road joins the main Chios to Volissos road (*see 'Northwest of the Island' for continuation of the itinerary from this point*).

To the south from the junction with the road from Avgónyma, the coast road heads 11km south to Vessa (*see next section*), passing the protected and sandy **bay of Lithí**

(6km) where there is a small harbour, good bathing and several fish tavernas, well-known for their fresh locally-caught fish. The bay is the alluvial mouth of a small fertile plain to the south which was the '*kambos*' for the small community of **Lithí**, on the hillside to the southeast. The village has enviable sunset views. Andreas Syngros, the 19th century philanthropist and banker who was instrumental in financing the completion of the Corinth Canal in 1893, was from this village; his Athenian residence is now the Greek Foreign Ministry and the principal artery from Athens to Faliron and Piraeus, 'Syngrou Avenue', is named after him.

SOUTHERN CHIOS &
THE MASTIC VILLAGES

This itinerary follows, in clockwise direction, the loop-road southwest from Chios town, via Armólia, Pyrgí, Mestá, and back to Chora via Véssa and Chalkeió. There are three detours off the main road: (1) to Panaghia Sikeliá and the area between the road and the coast at Katarráktis (east); (2) to the area of Kalamotí, Emporeió and Dótia (south); and (3) to the site of Ancient Phanai (southwest).

Twelve kilometres southwest of Chora, and 1km after passing the turning (south) for the villages of Myrmingi and Didyma, a small branch road bears left to the south towards Kalamotí, and runs along a ridge amid groves of mature mastic trees.

Detour 1: Panaghia Sikeliá to Katarráktis

Just over a kilometre after leaving the main road, the ruined **base of a circular tower** can be seen to the left of the road, in a field. The construction, while bearing similarities (in form, diameter and position) to the many Hellenistic towers of the Aegean area, does not have the masonry typical of such buildings and probably represents the remains of a late mediaeval watchtower, designed for signalling and for the protection of the area's valuable mastic groves. At 2.5km the picturesque ruins of the **monastery of the Panaghia Sikeliá** come into view on a rise to the right (west).

The 13th century *catholicon* of the monastery survives—reroofed and virtually bare in the interior. The interest here is in the characteristic Chiot **brick-decoration**, which runs throughout the building, alternating with courses of stone blocks, delineating a series of blind arcades, and creating the window arches of the octagonal drum; the decorative work is most varied at the east end and northwest corner. The brick designs incorporate small, hollow, cross-shaped elements which, because of their similarity to the crimped mouth of a certain kind of water jug, are called '***phialostomia***' ('bottle-mouths') and were a particularly popular kind of decoration on Chios. They are made by pinching circular rings of wet clay into a cross-design before firing. They are both decorative and functional, helping to ventilate the walls.

The area to the east, between Panaghia Sikeliá and the coast at the pleasant sea-side village of **Katarráktis** is a fertile lowland of hills and valleys given over to the cultivation of olive, mulberry (for silk production) and, above all, mastic trees. The name 'Katarráktis', meaning 'water-fall', comes from the earlier settlement now referred to as 'Palaio Katarráktis', which is at the head of the deep valley southwest of the modern village, at a confluence of streams and waterfalls coming down a series of small ravines. This is reached by taking the road for Pagída and Kiní southwest from Katarráktis, past the rebuilt church of the **Panaghia Rouchouniótissa**, which sits amongst its ruined 17th century convent buildings in a hollow to the north of the road: 1km (south) after Rouchouniótissa, a left turn leads into the area of **Palaio Katarráktis**. The road passes Aghia Hermioni, on the edge of a narrow ravine, and descends to **Aghios Ioannis Argentis**, an abandoned church and monastery set amongst groves of olives and fruit trees. Only the decorated narthex of the church dates from the original 14th century structure; the rest was rebuilt in the 17th century and subsequently abandoned. Fragments of the marble *templon*, and a discarded millstone, remain as testimony of its former activity. There are a great many rural, stone churches in this area and the scattered villages conserve a number of fine stone houses of the 18th and 19th centuries. (*End of detour*)

Armólia (19.5km from Chios) is the centre for a production of decorated ceramics. One kilometre northwest of the village is the 15th century **castle of Apolichnes** (*reached by a steep track from the north end of the village*), built by Girolamo Giustiniani in 1446 as part of a systematic plan by the Genoese occupiers for fortifying and protecting the valuable southern territory of the island. The fortress, enclosed by double ramparts, was large enough to afford temporary protection to the locals in case of attack. It still preserves its Great Tower, or 'keep', and a number of smaller defensive and look-out towers in the walls. To the south of Armólia extends the fertile valley of Kalamotí.

Detour 2: Kalamoti, Emporeió and Dótia

A kilometre southwest of the village of Kalamotí (*700m south from the southwest corner of the village, then 300m west to the top of the hill*) is the solitary church of the **Panaghia Agrelopoúsena**, now deprived of the monastery buildings which must once have surrounded it. The church was a 14th century dependency of *Nea Moni*, but the presence of Early Christian spolia nearby and of a fine section of **ancient cornice-moulding** with palmette design, incorporated in the building over the west door, may indicate earlier places of worship, possibly on this same panoramic site. Although predominantly a stone structure, the brick elements which are included have been put to constantly varying designs. The simple vaulted space of the interior is animated with blind arcades along the lateral walls and the scant remains of **wall-paintings**: the best preserved area of 14th century paintings is in the domed narthex, where the figures of the donors of the church remain; the name of one, Irene Mentoni, is legible.

South of Kalamotí, a fertile agricultural plain extends to the coast at **Kómi**; this is probably the oldest consistently cultivated area of Chios, which provided food for the island's earliest settlements around the protected harbour of **Emporeió** at its southern extremity. The harbour is marked by a hill to the west—ideal as an acropolis—and by another, higher mountain (today's Prophitis Elías hill) to its north and east; with a source of fresh-water in addition, directly behind the bay, the site was an obvious choice for settlement.

The importance of the **ancient site of *Emporeios*** derives from the antiquity, variety and continuity of settlement here; the excavations have also provided interesting information about early ancient dwellings. The various points of archaeological interest are spread over the whole area.

Excavations at the neck of the west promontory have revealed settlement remains beginning as early as the 5th millennium BC: no fewer than 10 subsequent phases have been distinguished by archaeologists, of which Phase III (late 3rd millennium BC) is the first to have had a strong defensive wall. Obsidian debitage is evidence that there were trading links with the Cyclades from early on. Mycenaean finds show that settlement continued until the end of the Bronze Age. When the island was re-colonised by Ionians from *Histiaia* on Euboea in the 8th century BC, the site they chose for settlement was not the previous one, but the slopes of the hill to the east and north instead which was to function ultimately as their acropolis. Here they constructed the sanctuary and temple of their patron goddess, Athena; while below, by the harbour, a sanctuary to Artemis was established. Between the two, stretched the inhabited town with its simple residences. Thucydides (VIII.24) appears to refer to the settlement as *Leukonion*. The area was populated in Roman times—when a fortress was erected on the summit of the promontory to the west of the harbour—and in Early Christian times, when the temple of Artemis was dismantled and used as a quarry to build an Early Christian basilica, whose baptismal font (still visible today) was beside the same water source which had supplied the very earliest settlements here, nearly 5,000 years before.

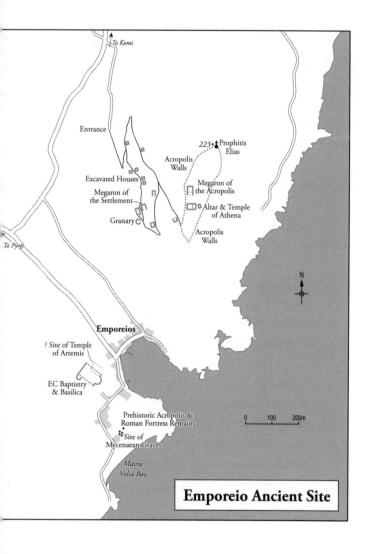

Emporeio Ancient Site

The road from Kómi to Emporeió passes below the entrance to the Archaeological Site on the south slopes of the hill of Prophitis Elias (open daily, 8.30–7 in summer; 9–one hour before sunset in winter). First excavated and published by John Boardman and the British School of Archaeology between 1951–54, the hillside today is laid out as a manicured archaeological park with concrete walkways and suggested itineraries. The visitor encounters principally four types of architecture on the site: temple, *megaron*, simple dwelling, and storage-house. The focus of the ancient town was the temple of Athena, which sits at the top of the site, within a **walled acropolis** encompassing the summit and the southern shoulder of the hill of Prophitis Elias.

Development of the temple of Athena

In the earliest phase (8th century BC) there was only a rectangular altar ('Altar A') here and a *peribolos* defining the sacred area. The first temple was built in the 6th century BC. It would have been a flat-roofed, rectangular building with a porch: it enclosed and covered the 8th century BC altar—the sanctuary's most sacred spot—and housed the cult image. A new external altar ('Altar B') was now built for communal cult: this is the long rectangular structure placed, a short distance away, parallel to the north side of the temple—an unusual position, since altars were nearly always to be found to the east of the front of a temple. Immediately following its destruction in the early 4th century BC, the temple was rebuilt in the form visible today, this time with a pitched roof instead of the flat roof: a new altar ('Altar C')was created, in front of the east entrance, but at a curiously skewed angle to the temple building.

The masonry of the temple visible today has the characteristic precision of Hellenistic (4th century BC) construction. Its magnificently panoramic position is characteristic of Greek temple-sites of all periods. Inside the confines of the temple, the stone **base for the cult statue** can be seen in the southwest corner and the remains of the earliest, 8th century BC **altar** are next to it, just to the north.

The settlement

From in front of the temple, what remains of the 800m circuit of **walls of the acropolis** can be seen flanking the ridge to east and west as they rise up to the summit. Almost contiguous with the western wall, and just north of the temple, is the *megaron* of the 8th century BC—a long rectangular hall, preceded by a porch supported on wooden columns whose stone bases can still be seen: this was the official residence of the ruler and would also have served as a council chamber for the elders. The lowest courses of its perimeter-wall are of massive blocks settled amongst pieces of the bedrock; on top of these, the walls are made of smaller stone pieces. They would have been finished with plastered mud-brick at the top, and covered with a flat roof, supported on a line of three central wooden columns. On the slopes of the hill below the walls, a number of houses of great simplicity have been uncovered: mostly single-chambered **dwellings** with a stone bench along the walls for sleeping, sometimes a semi-interred storage area and a single threshold giving on to an external courtyard, often shared by more than one such house. In the southwest corner, one building distinguishes itself by its unusual circular form (c. 5.2m in diameter) and by the presence of a storage jar beside the door: this may represent a communal **storehouse**. The humble simplicity of every construction here is striking.

A short distance (40–50m) up the road that rises to the west of the harbour, a signed track leads (*right*) into a field below some modern houses where there are the remains of a late 6th century AD **Palaeochristian basilica** and **baptismal font**. The cruciform font, still with its marble revetment of the steps leading down into the pool, is protected by a modern circular stone structure. To the east of this, and now much overgrown, are traces of the basilica to which the baptistery was adjoined; a deep apse with

mosaic pavement can be distinguished. The area is full
of finely-worked masonry and architectural decorations
taken from ancient buildings by the port and incorporated randomly in the foundations and walls of the basilica.
The road continues up over the hill to the southwest of
the harbour and drops down almost immediately to the
'**Black Beach**' of Mávra Vólia Bay where, between the sea
and ochre-coloured cliffs behind, an extraordinary vol-
canic strand of evenly sized, black pebbles stretches for a
good hundred metres. A different variety of colours, no
less unusual, are to be seen at the **bay of Phokí**, 300m by
path to the south along the shore.

On the Emporeió to Pyrgí road (1.2km northwest of
Emporeió), a turning back to the south leads to the Genoese **tower of Dótia** (2.2km) which constituted the impressive, central keep of a fortified settlement in the midst
of a wide area of mastic trees. At the centre of the villages
of Mestá and Pyrgí there are similar towers, suggesting that
Dótia, too, would have been a similar but smaller mediaeval village: although most is now rubble, the walls and corner bastions of the surrounding settlement are still visible.
The tower itself, which stands to almost 20m in height and
shows vestiges of three interior floors supported by brick
vaults, is similar in design and material to the Genoese
towers on the north coast of Samothrace which also date

from the first years of the 15th century. The tower here is slightly larger and has greater elegance in the slight talus at its base. Like its predecessors, the Classical and Hellenistic towers of the Aegean, it was a multi-purpose construction, providing protection for agricultural land and, at the same time, functioning as a look-out and signalling tower.

The road back north from Dótia leads through undulating hills covered with **mastic groves** towards the most famous of the so-called 'Mastic Villages', Pyrgí (7km), where the main loop-road from Chora is rejoined. (*End of detour.*)

THE MASTIC VILLAGES

The hilly landscape of the south of Chios is dominated by the cultivation of mastic trees, and the villages in this area were the centres of production for the gum. Mastic never was or could be a large-scale industry, but the demand was constant from Byzantine times on and its importance to Chios lay in the fact that this area of the island was the only place in the Mediterranean where the tree had been successfully cultivated and cropped. Byzantium and Italy were the principal markets for the product, later to be superseded by Turkey and the Orient. Most of the villages in this area probably have Byzantine origins, but it was under Genoese rule in the 14th and 15th centuries that they were properly organised into a community of settlements, with special administration and special architectural design so as to protect themselves from the predations of piracy. This was done with the methodical determination and pragmatism for which the Genoese were (and are) well-known. The villages, still referred to generically as the *Mastichochória*, have certain features in common: they lie inland and are hidden from view from the sea; they are walled for protection; they are built around a central fortified tower, which formed the ultimate safe-refuge for the inhabitants and their precious product in case of attack; they have the tight-knit plan of narrow streets and passageways typical of the mother city of 14th century Genoa, and in which the backs of the outer ring of houses is one with the enceinte of walls. The villages' special administrative privileges, put in place originally by the Genoese, were confirmed and enlarged when the Turks took control of the island in the 16th century; so important was the mastic trade and supply to Istanbul, that the Mastic Villages were specifically spared the gruesome Ottoman reprisals of 1822 which so badly affected the rest of the island. The Mastic Villages are canonically over 20 in number, some (Armólia and Kalamotí) mentioned already: for the purposes of this guide, the four finest examples are looked at in particular—Pyrgí, Olýmpi, Mestá and Véssa.

MASTIC

The evergreen mastic tree (*Pistacia lentiscus*) is low, dense and 'sculpted' in form, with dark leathery leaves and a rough, corrugated bark from which it spontaneously weeps a pale yellow, largely odourless, resin or hardened sap. This 'weeping' can be promoted by making incisions (called 'hurts') in the trunk and branches of the mature tree and by harvesting the resin from June through to September; 'hurting' too young a tree, however, inhibits its growth. The sap coagulates as it drips from the cuts and is collected, rinsed in barrels, and dried: a second cleaning is done by hand. At its prime, a tree will yield 4.5kg of mastic gum in one season. Many varieties of mastic trees grow wild throughout the Mediterranean area; but it is only on Chios that the local *Pistacia lentiscus chia* variety has become 'domesticated' and responded to intensive cultivation.

Dioscorides—observant writer on plants and herbs of the 1st century AD—mentions the mastic gum as used for attaching false eyelashes to eyelids

(*Materia Medica*, I. 91): it was also known in Antiquity as a treatment for duodenal ulcer and heart-burn. Christopher Columbus believed it to be a cure for cholera. But the most enduring quality of the gum has been its power, when masticated, to neutralise and to scent the breath. This was widely appreciated in the harems of Arabia and Turkey; 18th century reports suggest that the Ottoman Sultan kept half of the annual harvest from Chios for the *Seraglio* in Top Kapı—a quantity equivalent to about 125 tons.

The Genoese were the first to see the commercial potential of intensive production of mastic, and it was for this, more than any other product of the island, that they took such immense pains to protect the island from piracy and secure the villages which produced the precious resin. Under Ottoman occupation this protection was maintained and the villages were given further special privileges, forming a separate administrative region linked directly with the Sublime Porte through elected representation. It was commonly said that the women of the Sultan's harem, who used the mastic also as a beauty cosmetic, had Chios under their protection. As with the production of any valuable commodity, limitations were put on the producers and the penalties for stealing mastic, first laid down by the Genoese and then perpetuated by the Turks, were severe physical disfigurement.

The flavour of the gum is initially bitter, but after a few minutes of chewing it softens and releases a light, cedar-like freshness into the mouth which remains for about 15 to 20 minutes. The gum has a variety of medicinal, culinary and practical applications; it is soluble in oil of turpentine and was the commonest varnish for pictures in the 19th century; Rubens favoured it as a stabiliser in paints; it is an ingredient in many kinds of incense, was employed in dentistry for temporary fillings, and, in the refined world of Ottoman cuisine, it is still used in the preparation of true Turkish Delight, or *rahat lokum*, and as a binding agent with oil, lemon juice and spices to coat the outer surface of the traditional *döner kebab*. On Chios its distinctive flavour can be sampled in many ways; principally in the local grape spirit, '*Masticha*', or else in a variety of *gliká tou koutalíou*, or 'spoon sweets', submerged in a glass of ice-cold water to assuage thirst. Something of a renaissance in the marketing of mastic has occurred in the last decade, and it is now sold as a nostalgically packaged luxury item, both on the island and further afield in Greece.

PYRGI

The largest and most important of the Mastic Villages—because of its central position in the area—is *Pyrgí (23km from Chora). The village is most vividly memorable for its idiosyncratic grey and white **decorations on the façades** of the houses, executed in a *sgraffito* technique, i.e. scraping away the outer white surface of the rendering to expose the grey *pozzolana* (or cement today) in predetermined geometric patterns—referred to locally as '*xysta*', ('scrapings' or 'grazings'). Although this is found elsewhere in the villages, nowhere has it reached a comparable complexity and ubiquity as in Pyrgí. Combined with the delicate wrought-iron work of the balconies, and occasionally set off by foliage and flowers in the narrow streets, the effect is unusual and unforgettable. The ubiquitous spread of the elaborate decoration is a recent phenomenon, dating from the turn of the last century; but its origins almost certainly go back to mediaeval

Genoa, where it was used sparingly on the fronts of patrician houses.

The town originally had one principal entrance—a gateway on the north side, which is the most appropriate way to approach the town. Ahead is the central *plateia*, grouped around the large, modern church of the **Koimisis tis Theotokou**. To the south, at the highest point of the town is the three storey '*pyrgos*' or '**Great Tower**', now partially ruined and lower than its original imposing height; it stands at the heart of the town, with an empty 'cordon sanitaire' around, which separates it from the dense network of streets beyond. This was the refuge in case of attack, and was originally entered by a wooden bridge which was then removed and pulled inside.

One of the island's loveliest and most important churches—the 14th century *church of the Aghii Apostoli—is entered down an arched alley off the east side of the central square. (*Open daily 8.30–3 except Mon.*) The approaching passageway allows only a confined and focused view of its striking **west front**: the beautiful masonry of the walls, with each stone-block carefully framed by brick tiles; the classical marble door-frame with carved decorations, surmounted by an arched niche of the same size above—now deprived of its painting, but still preserving the delicate border of *phialostomia* (tiny open crosses of terracotta) which surrounds it; and the magnificent **drum and cupola** which rises as high again above, with undulating eaves, decorative brick dentils, and broad window-frames composed of concentric arches of brick patterns. Like the Panaghia Krina, this is deeply influenced by the architecture and design of the *catholicon* at *Nea Moni*; but it is no mere copy. Its form is more compact, and its surface more decorated, but there is less of the aristocratic stylisation in its design. Since the building was renovated in 1564 by a certain 'Simeon', later Bishop of Chios, according to the inscription above the door, it is hard to be certain of its original date of construction: a mid-14th century date is generally agreed, but its style suggests that it may have been put up as much as a hundred years earlier. A walk around the exterior (*access from either of the parallel streets to north or south*) reveals the inventiveness and constant variety of the **brick decoration**. Inside the church is covered with **wall-paintings**, signed and dedicated in a panel on the north wall by the Cretan artist, Antonios Domestichos, in 1665: he was working, it might be recalled, a full two generations after his fellow islander, El Greco. The gentle but intentful face of the ***Pantocrator*** in the cupola is stylistically far in time and distance from the 11th century Constantinopolitan world of the solemn figures of the mosaics at *Nea Moni*.

As always with late Byzantine painting, the accent here is on narrative content and decorative pattern: this is particularly noticeable in the two memorable scenes of the *Ascension* and of the *Harrowing of Hell* on respectively the south and north walls of the crossing. The latter ingeniously incorporates an overlay of iconographic aspects of the Resurrection, in the open tomb and the slumbering Roman guardsmen below.

A little over two kilometres west of Pyrgí, along the branch-road southwest to Phaná, is the tiny chapel of **Aghia Marina**, to the north side of the road. The modern construction is built on ancient foundations and incorporates ancient masonry in its structure: it is probably the site of a small 5th century BC sanctuary, related to the presence of the main sanctuary of Apollo *Phanaios* (*see pp. 95–96*) further southwest at the coast.

OLYMPI

West of Pyrgí and spread low in the floor of a wide valley is the quieter village of **Olýmpi** (31km from Chios; 7.5km west of Pyrgi), which like Pyrgí was laid out in its present form in the 14th century by the Genoese. There is no access into its squat, fortress-like form from the south and east sides; the main entrance is once again in the north walls, by way of a **monumental gateway** which preserves its original stone frame. From here the cobbled street leads under a passage decorated with xysta to the central square, where the rectangular **fortress-tower** has survived to a substantial height. Even though it is the centre of the settlement, there is deliberately no axial access to it. To the north of the tower are the churches of **Aghia Paraskeví** and of the **Taxiarches**—simple, low and roofed with schist tiles. The former, which appears to be built over a burial site or ossuary, may predate the Genoese rebuilding of the town: the date of 1742 inscribed over the door refers to a later restoration of the church which included the addition of the carved wooden **iconostasis**.

Detour 3: Ancient *Phanai* and Olýmpi Cave

A short distance east of Olýmpi, a road branches south towards the coast, and leads after 5.5km to **Olýmpi Cave** (*open daily, except Mon, May 11–5; June–Oct 10–8*). Discovered as recently as 1985, this is a small cave between 60 and 70m in depth at certain points, with particularly fine '**filigree' stalactite and stalagmite formations** (still actively forming) of a prevailing, yellowy-reddish hue. A small natural entrance lets sunlight in from above. The cave is estimated to be approximately 150 million years old. A kilometre below, the road ends at the church of the Aghia Dýnami, beside a ruined mediaeval watchtower overlooking a protected inlet of turquoise water.

At a junction along the same road and approximately mid-way between Olýmpi and the Cave (approximately 3km from each), a track leads off, almost parallel and slightly to the east, to Phaná, the site of **Ancient *Phanai*** (also accessible by 5.5km of partially metalled road, directly from Pyrgí). As the track begins to approach the shore, a **spring-house** to the left which incorporates some finely-drafted pieces of classical masonry already gives an intimation of an ancient presence in the area. The archaeological site, first systematically explored by the British School of Archaeology and currently still under excavation, is 100m further on beside the chapel of **Aghios Theodoros** (marked on some maps as 'Aghia Markella') which is built over site of the **temple of Apollo *Phanaios***. This was primarily a place of cult, not an inhabited settlement; what is to be seen at the site gives little sense of the size, importance and longevity of the sanctuary, where finds from the Geometric period attest the worship of Apollo from as early as the 9th century BC. The name '*Phanai*', cognate with '*φαίνειν*' ('to appear'), suggests that the origin of the cult was a divine epiphany of some sort. As so often, there are many successive strata to the site. The *peribolos* of the earliest Geometric sanctuary (1), of which vestiges survive, was first replaced by an early 6th century BC, Archaic (2) **perimeter wall** constructed in irregular blocks of limestone. Not long after, in the later 6th century BC, it was rebuilt in a large, regular, interlocking style of masonry (3), a section of which can be seen some way in front and below the west of the modern church, to the side of the track as it climbs up from the shore. The foundations and the corner of the **platform of the temple** from this period can be seen to the northeast of the church. (The tiny silver-gilt figurine of a helmeted warrior in the Archaeological Museum, which was found here, relates to this period, as do the many fine 6th century BC architectural fragments displayed in the collection.) This Archaic temple was perhaps destroyed in the aftermath of the unsuccessful Ionian revolt of 494 BC, and rebuilt at least once (4) in the late 5th or early 4th century BC. It is from this period that the beautiful masonry, visible to the south and east of the church by the road, dates. These are mostly blocks in a bluish-grey limestone with rustication and precise double-drafting at the edges. A single **column base**, in a different white marble, lies nearby, with a design of concentric horizontal flutes or channels similar to that found at the temple of Hera on Samos. Finally, an Early Christian church (5), the foundations of whose apse are visible to the east of the present church, was constructed

here from the stones of the temple. The story ends somewhat bathetically with the modern chapel (6) of Aghios
Theodoros, whose apse conserves a small, carved capital
as its altar table. The shoreline has in all probability re-
ceded; the pagan temple would have stood on a high ter-
raced platform, directly above the water of a deeper inlet
of the sea, from which flights of steps (visible in places)
would have given access to the sanctuary. The site is particularly peaceful and atmospheric in the evening light. In
May the dunes of the beach are home to the Holy Orchid,
Orchis sancta. Amongst the birds that frequent the undis-
turbed, mixed habitats here are the Little bittern, Water
rail, and—easier to spot, though elusive—the Kingfisher.
(*End of detour.*)

MESTA

Mestá, which lies 3.7km northwest of Olýmpi, is linked
by a pleasant, well-signed **footpath** which crosses the low
hills that separate the two villages; it affords glimpses in
the Spring of many wild orchids: *Orchis anatolica*, as well
as the much rarer *Ophrys fleischmanii*.

Mestá is perhaps the most mediaeval in aspect of the
Mastic Villages and conserves clearly the pentagonal shape
of its original, 14th century plan. The **circuit of walls** and

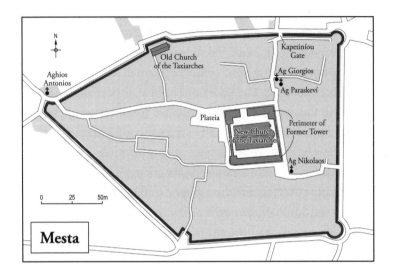

Mesta

gates are well-preserved; so too are the fine **circular bastions**, especially that of the northeastern corner. The habitation is densely packed and low, and the streets are narrow and labyrinthine, giving the village an airless feel—as if constantly awaiting a siege. Many of the alleys pass under buildings and through passageways; this linked each building to the next, so that the network of contiguous roofs which it created allowed free movement at the level of the tops of the buildings and the surrounding walls in times of attack and danger. Everything revolves around the large central square, dominated by the disproportionate size of the **church of the Taxiarches** at its centre; it stands on the site of the original Genoese tower, which was demolished when the church was erected in 1868. A small surviving section of the mediaeval tower's walls is visible below the old belfry to the west. Beside the doors of the west entrance of the church, a fragment of ancient stone clearly **inscribed with a decree** has been immured in the wall. The surviving 14th century churches stand to the northeast and southeast of the square; only **Aghios Giorgios** and **Aghios Panteleimon** (northeast) preserve some late painting in the interior, in poor condition.

The former **old church of the Taxiarches**, which lies northwest of the central square just inside the northern perimeter wall, presents an interesting assemblage of buildings. Entered through an **ornate gateway** in the rich red stone of Thymianá, is a small enclosure once occupied by monastic buildings. At the centre was a vaulted, single-aisled, basilica church; in 1794 the church was enlarged by the addition of a *parecclesion* to the north, creating a much wider interior space which is now divided by a low arcade supported on columns and capitals. The fine **carved iconostasis** was added a little later in 1883.

The shallow fertile valley to the west of Mestá—sown with isolated stone churches, mostly of the 18th century and sited variously beside a well, on an eminence or by a stand of mastic trees—provides a pleasant walk among groves of olive and fruit trees down to the shore at **Merik-ounta Bay**.

At the top of the rise 600m north of Mestá, a track branches left for Skouriá and the **Livadíou watchtower**, which dominates and protects the bay of Mestá and its harbour of Liménas. The 14th century cylindrical grey-stone tower still conserves some of its crenellations and machicolations at the rim: the only access—a stone framed window—is a good 7m above ground level.

WATCHTOWERS ON CHIOS

The long rugged coastline of Chios has a protective girdle of watchtowers. They are almost 50 in number and punctuate the island's promontories regularly in a complete circuit. Many survive in good condition, especially in the west and southwest of the island. A number of these towers, referred to as *vigles* or *phriktories*, are Byzantine in origin, but the majority date from the Genoese occupation of the 14th and 15th centuries. The organisational thoroughness of the Genoese has been noted elsewhere in this chapter; this went beyond the political and commercial structures which they created for the island's economy and administration, and was underpinned by a formidable military security system of which the towers were an integral part. This was an expression of the value they set upon their possession of Chios—its strategic position in trade with the Orient and the Black Sea, and its unique production of mastic—a market the Genoese were set on monopolising. The walled and fortified villages of the Mastic area, the chief fortress at the port of Chios, the critical look-out points over shipping routes, such as Avgónyma and Anávatos, and the coastal signalling towers or *vigles*, were all part of an integrated defence system of impressive design. In this strategic chess-game, the *vigles* were the front line of defence—the pawns on the board: their form is somewhat similar. They are the descendants of the Hellenistic towers, such as that at *Drakanon* on Ikaria—only they are constructed in rough stone rubble bound in mortar, rather than in ashlar masonry. Their strength was increased by the fact that they were solid to at least half their height. For this reason the only aperture—a cross between a door and a window—was rarely lower than 6 or 7m above ground level. This meant that access to the interior was only by rope-ladder and grappling hook. Only a small garrison of three or four men was needed to man the towers whose job was to relay messages by pigeon or fire signals; this related principally to any approaching danger, such as pirates or enemy forces; but it also importantly included giving vital notice to the markets of the main city of the arrival of commercial vessels of Genoese ownership.

VESSA, AGHIOS GIORGIOS SIKOUSIS & THE ROAD BACK TO CHORA

Other watchtowers in less good state of preservation can be seen from the road beyond Liménas as it follows the indented coast. Thirteen kilometres beyond Mestá, at the top of a limestone ravine, dotted with stone chapels and hidden from view from the sea, is the village of **Elata**; after crossing a rocky plateau, the road descends sharply to *****Véssa** (17km from Mestá), in many ways the most attractive and unchanged of the Mastic Villages. The centre of the village is reached at the end of an avenue of eucalyptus trees.

The settlement, hidden from view until the last moment, straddles the fertile floor of a shallow valley between two limestone ridges. The **stone houses** along its compact and logical grid of narrow streets, have many of the elements typical of the 14th century Genoese 'masterplan' for the villages of the area: narrow stone relieving arches above windows and doors; protruding machicolations and turrets; balconies supported on small arches; upper floors which cross the streets creating covered passageways; storage areas on the lower levels; towers, gates and fortifications. Concrete has hardly intruded into the stone and mortar buildings at any point. Many of the fine structures around the attractive *plateia*, though mediaeval in origin, bear the dates of their reconstruction or renovation—typically the 1820s and 1830s.

Véssa is 18km from Chios town by the remaining (northern) sector of the southern loop road. Seven kilometres east, after crossing the watershed amidst pines and limestone outcrops, the port and the straits between Chios and Turkey come dramatically into view at the village of **Aghios Giorgios Sikousis** ('rich in figs'), which is built along a ridge of the mountain, lined with the remains of windmills. Although this is not one of the canonical Mastic Villages, it is a mediaeval settlement whose plan can be seen at the north end of the ridge, around and to the south of the patronal church. Vaulted passageways, gates, and even a substantial part of the original **medi-aeval fortress** tower still stand, unselfconsciously woven together with 19th century buildings. The main church of St George was, like the earlier Panaghia Krina in the valley below, a 12th century building strongly influenced by the *catholicon* of *Nea Moni*: it was completely rebuilt in the late 18th century, and preserves a memory of its former self in the brick drum and cupola. Above the main west door, a fine **decorative slab** of green, Thessalian marble has been preserved from the earlier church; while in front a large area of 19th century *chochlakia* pavement extends to the west.

Like Aghios Giorgios Sikousis, the tiny village of **Ziphiás**, 3km further east towards Chora, was also a walled and gated mediaeval village on a smaller scale: remains of its fortifications are still visible. The south door of the main church of **Aghia Paraskeví** conserves the elaborately carved door-posts and lintel block of an earlier 18th century predecessor.

One last, fine example of the decorative brick-work typical of the early churches of mediaeval Chios can be seen near the next village to the east, **Chalkeío** (6km from Chora), above and to the left (north) of the eastern extremity of the habitation. The elaborate window-surrounds and decorative blind niches at the east end of the church of **Aghios Ioannis** are part of the original, 14th century construction. In the 19th century the surrounding monastery buildings were lost and the steeply pitched roof was rebuilt. Many ruined **brick kilns** are visible in the area between here and Chora, and it must have been the predecessors of these that supplied the material for *Nea Moni* and for the many mediaeval churches on the island that copied its design.

THE NORTHWEST OF THE ISLAND

VOLISSOS

Thucydides (VIII. 24) refers to '*Boliskos*', which must be the ancient city on this site: although little is to be seen today of an ancient precursor, it would be unusual if such a site—with its natural harbour, an acropolis hill, a fertile plain for cultivation, a good supply of water, and its proximity to the island of *Psyra* (Psará)—had not attracted settlement in Antiquity. The town was the home of the *Homeridai*, a clan that claimed descent from Homer, whose name had always been associated with the island. The acropolis hill is now occupied by a fine **Genoese castle**, the harbour, **Limniá** (1.5km from the town), still functions, and the watercourses have, until recently, fed a series of **watermills** of varying age, in the stretch between Volissós and Mánagros Bay. (The mills are visitable by taking a pleasant route by foot, signed 'Mánagros', from below the eastern side of Volissós; this is one of the richest areas on the island for the display of wildflowers in the spring). What distinguishes Volissós from many other Chiot villages is the variety of styles of architecture: in a short distance there are simple **neoclassical** residences, **Ottoman-style** houses with overhanging wooden balconies, and **mediaeval** stone houses; the latter predominate increasingly as one climbs up towards the *kastro*. The castle was a key element in the late 14th century fortification of the island undertaken by the Genoese, and, though ruined, has been little modified through time. The circuit of walls with six round, irregularly placed, corner bastions, encloses churches, cisterns and other buildings in a large, trapezoid area. The **fortress tower**, or 'keep', in the southwest corner has survived in relatively good condition. The tradition that the castle was built by Belisarius in the 6th century is almost certainly legend; but the remarkable 11th century historian and imperial princess, Anna Comnena, mentions Volissos and its castle in her *Alexiad*. What she was referring to was probably demolished by the Genoese builders when they began the construction of the existing fort.

From the harbour of Limniá a road follows the coast west to the bay and monastery of **Aghia Markella** (4.5km)—site of the martyrdom of the young virgin saint of the (?)16th century (there is much ambiguity about the dates of her life) from Volissós whose feast day, 22 July, is the most widely celebrated in the island's religious calendar. A simple cross at the water's edge marks the point—at the far end of the beach—where the saint died reputedly at the hands of her possessed father: two springs of therapeutic water rise at the site, whose high mineral content has coloured the rock a deep red—symbolic of the blood of her martyrdom.

THE WEST COAST TO AGHIO GALA

The main road which heads northwest from Volissós winds through a wide sandstone landscape different in vegetation from elsewhere on the island: the villages, set athwart the ravines of mountain torrents, are open and panoramic, with the curious exception of **Melaniós**, which is huddled out of sight in a seemingly subterranean dip, at the western tip of the island. Twenty two kilometres from Volissós, the road turns into the steep valley of **Aghio Gála**, the site of the earliest human habitation on the island so far discovered. The village itself is built high up along the ridge of a projecting spur, with clear views to Psará across a famously windy stretch of water: the rock beneath is perforated with a network of **deep caves**, entered from the cliff of the gorge above the watercourse below. It is here that human settlers from as early as 6000 BC have left artefacts relating to their habitation or worship; the tiny rectangular plaque of clay, modelled and incised in the form of a man's face—which constitutes the earliest representational find in the Chios Archaeological Museum—was found here. The combination of shelter, security and numinousness afforded by the cave has meant that cult has continued here intermittently from the Neolithic Age, into historic antiquity—from Archaic through to Roman—and on into the Christian era. Today it is the Christian buildings which are visible; the cave entrance is now closed by the 14th century church of the **Panaghia Aghiogalousena** ('Virgin of the Sacred Milk') whose apse and elongated cupola are in the typical style of late mediaeval Chios. (*Generally kept locked, outside July & Aug. Key should be obtained from the guardian who lives in the square of the village above.*) The church was restored early in the last century, when the Lindos-ware and 'Willow pattern' ceramic plates were immured in its exterior: the principal interest of the interior is the intricately **carved iconostasis** and the one remaining area of painting in the apse figuring the Virgin '*platytera*' (with open arms). Around the church are grouped the abandoned hermitage buildings, dating probably from the 17th century. Standing entirely within the cave, reached through the church of the Panaghia, is the contemporaneous **chapel of St Anne**, with wall-paintings in deteriorating condition. The cave penetrates for 200m into the rock, through a series of linked chambers with active stalagmite and stalactite formation: it is probably the milky appearance of the calciferous water which moistens the upper surface of the stalactites that has given rise to the epithet of the Virgin here.

The houses at the southern extremity of the village of Aghio Gála, beyond the rudimentary *plateia*, are clustered within the walls of what was obviously a tiny **fortress**. The steps which lead down from here to the cave and the churches pass by the ancient church of **Aghios Thalelaios**—a simple, early mediaeval, vaulted stone structure which incorporates in its walls a number of blocks and pieces of stone from an earlier construction. Its simple interior contains a finely-carved, early 18th century **oak-wood iconostasis**, which must be one of the oldest examples of this local style and craft on the island. The **wall-paintings**, which probably date from the 16th century, are much less well-preserved and have suffered from partial defacing (especially the eyes) during the *tourkokratia*: the scenes of the *Life of Christ* on the north side of the vault are the best preserved. Both a footpath from the valley below, and a track from a point on the main road 500m east of the village, lead southeast to the deserted **hamlet of Aghios Ioannis** (30 mins/2km). The homonymous church, which lies below the cluster of deserted, dark-stoned houses, also has an early **carved wooden iconostasis**, in similar local style to that in Aghios Thalelaios.

THE NORTH COAST TO AGHIASMATA

The route east, which winds from ravine to ravine, high above the largely deserted north coast, is densely forested and well-watered. In Antiquity this area produced '***Ariousion* wine**'—the most famous wine to be produced on an island already famed for its wines in general. The Chiots of the Classical era were over-fond of it according to Aristophanes, who contrasted them with the sober inhabitants of the island of *Keos* (Kea). A distant descendant of this wine is still to be had in the attractive village of **Kouroúnia** (33km from Volissós). There is epigraphic evidence of a cult of Hercules at Kouroúnia; and at Aphrodísia (38km), the name itself suggests a cult of the goddess of love. From Aphrodísia, a branch road plunges down into the ravine towards Aghiásmata. The small community of Kéramos at the head of the valley, 2.3km below, still conserves some of the ruined mine-buildings associated with the extraction of antimony. This is an area generally rich in minerals and the **hot thermal waters** which rise by the sea at **Aghiásmata** (44.5km) derive their curative qualities from this. These therapeutic powers have been appreciated and used continuously since Byzantine times, if not for longer, and are mentioned with approval by visitors and writers from the 17th century on. This makes it

additionally sad that the place today has such an abandoned and uncared-for feel. The springs, where the water
rises at 68°C, are at the western edge of the beach, just
beyond the abandoned bath-house on the shore; the water is now pumped from a concrete hut over the springs
directly back to the Hydrotherapy Spa, which lies in the
floor of the valley, 500m to the south. At the moment, this
is only open from July to September; the curative waters
remain inaccessible for the rest of the year. In compensa-
tion, the cliffs nearby are good for collecting **samphire**.

By the direct route south along the valley between the
Amaní and Pelinnaíon massifs, Aghiásmata is only 19km
from Volissós. After the watershed above Aphrodísia, the
road descends with vistas across the wide spaces of the
central area of the island. The nature of this area has been
transformed by past fires and by the abandonment of a
number of the villages; as a result, a very different vegetation from before has grown up, followed by a different
fauna. These upland grassy areas are now the terrain of
the Woodchat shrike and of the rare **Cinereous bunting**,
a muted version of its commoner cousin, the Red-headed
bunting.

Near Nea Potamiá (7km from Volissós) are two of the
abandoned villages: **Paliá Potamiá**, 1km above its modern namesake to which the inhabitants have since moved;

and the evocative area of Tamárkou, or more accurately, **Ta Markou** (3.5km below, by the road to Pispiloúnta). This is a mediaeval settlement with fortress tower, churches, and roofless houses, overgrown with vegetation and abandoned since the beginning of the last century.

THE NORTHEAST OF THE ISLAND

VRONTADOS & THE KARDAMYLA VALLEY

Along the shore to its north, the town of Chios blends seamlessly into the area of **Vrontados**, which had already become a seaside retreat for Chiots who wanted the luxury of a villa in a garden close to the shore, by the time the arrival of refugees from Smyrna and Asia Minor in 1923 began to swell its borders. Suburban spread outside of the main town of Chios, between the 15th and the 19th centuries, had always been towards the south into Kambos; then, at the start of the 20th century, it moved towards the north here at Vrontados—favoured by the beautiful setting between the steep slope of Mount Aípos and the sea, and by clearer waters for bathing, freshened by the prevailing north-south current of the sea-channel.

The shore-line road passes the **bronze statue** and memorial to the *Lost Sailor*, by Thanassis Apartis (1899–1972). Apartis was from Smyrna, on the coast opposite, and, like his contemporary from Andros, Michalis Tombros, studied and worked extensively in Paris early in his life.

Vrontados ends, to the north, at the mouth of a ravine: at this site, between mountain and torrent and sea, a **sanctuary to Cybele** was established perhaps as early as the 6th century BC. Its remains are known as the ***Daskalópetra***, or 'Teacher's Stone', sometimes just referred to as '**Homer's Rock**' because it was long considered to be the spot where Homer taught his pupils the poet's art. The predominantly Ionic nature of the mixed dialect of Homer's epics has always been taken to suggest the poet's origins in this part of the Greek world, and Chios and Smyrna (modern Izmir) on the mainland opposite have traditionally had the strongest claims to have been his birthplace.

What the visitor sees here is an outcrop of limestone whose upper surfaces have been fashioned by hand into a terrace; in the middle of this is a roughly cuboid protrusion of the bedrock—originally a throne—on whose sides the very **eroded reliefs** of lions and (at the four lower corners) lions' claws can just be perceived. The throne faced due east; the knob of stone in the middle of the east face probably corresponds to the knees of the seated divinity. To one side, a raised lip of rock has been fashioned into the form of a **long stone bench**. The wild setting of the gorge, the overhanging mountains, the torrent and the shore, all combine to make a site typical of such ancient sanctuaries; the rock protrusion

was the **altar**, and the bench, a defining part of the ritual
area frequented by celebrants. The lion reliefs help to iden-
tify the cult as that of Cybele, the great mother-goddess of
Anatolia—mistress of wild nature, which was symbolised
by her ever-present attendant lions. Cybele, who was later
associated with and integrated into the Hellenic pantheon
as Demeter, was widely honoured on Chios, and this may
have been one of her principal sanctuaries. Archaeological
finds from this area (now in the museum in Chios) of votive offerings and inscriptions confirm the identity of the
cult: it took place in the open air, and often involved ecstatic
states, inducing prophetic rapture and insensibility to pain.
Cybele's strong presence on the island is witness to the rich
cross-fertilisation of different cults between east and west in
the early historic period in this part of the Aegean.

After a stretch of inhospitably rocky coast, the deep inlet and attractive waterfront of **Langáda** (15km) come
into view, with fertile land behind and around. Ancient
inscriptions and archaeological soundings have shown
that in the north area of the bay (now occupied by a military camp) was the sanctuary of Apollo *Delphinios* and
Artemis *Delphinia*. It was in this bay, following the revolt of Chios against Athens in 412 BC, that the Athenians
fortified their position after the capture of the island of

Oinousa and maintained a constant presence up until 406 BC.

A year-round water-taxi service runs between Langáda and the islands of Oinousses (4 nautical miles to the east in the channel between Chios and Turkey; *see below pp. 137–149*). Inland of Langáda a steep, cemented track climbs up through the village of Agrelopó to the deserted settlement of **Kidianta**, set in a valley to one side of a bare and impressive gorge. The village was a stronghold of the islanders' resistance to the German occupation during the Second World War. Beyond Kidianta, the track climbs further onto the bleak rock plateau above, with views across Oinousses and far into Turkey. On the saddle (c. 2km beyond Kidianta), dominated by a flat-topped tor to the east, scattered masonry and ancient remains have been located, which are believed to correspond to the site of Ancient *Koila*.

At 22km from Chora, the main road descends into the *valley of Kardámyla**, one of the island's most attractive corners with a long and little-explored history. Apart from the references to '*Koila*' and '*Kardamyle*' in Herodotus and Thucydides, there is epigraphic evidence of the cult of Zeus *Patröos* in a forested grove on Mount Pelinnaíon above the town, as well as of Dionysos *Actaios*, of Aphrodite *Kytheria*, and of Poseidon, in other parts of the territory at places yet to be pinpointed with precision. On a steep eminence directly to the south, stand the remains of the 15th century **Grías Castle**—essentially a small fortress, consisting of two towers of slightly differing form, linked by curtain walls and built over the site of earlier Hellenistic fortifications (*accessible by foot in 45 mins from Ano Kardámyla by signed footpaths*).

Recent settlement in the area is split between two nuclei—the picturesque hillside village of **Ano Kardámyla** above, and the administrative centre of **Mármaro** below, which clusters around the coastal inlet to the northeast: between the two, stretches the fertile '*kambos*', fed by the waters that descend from Mount Pelinnaíon through the upper village and into the valley. Kardámyla is predominantly mediaeval in character; from the attractive *plateia*, shaded by huge plane-trees, the steep, narrow streets of stone houses rise to the area of Spiliá which was the original settlement here. Mármaro, by contrast, is predominantly Ottoman and neoclassical in architecture, pleasingly grouped around the deep inlet with windmills at various points amongst the houses. On the waterfront is a another bronze sculpture by Thanassis Apartis (*see above*)—*The Unknown Sailor*. The name of the settlement—meaning 'marble'—would suggest the presence of quarries of some antiquity in the area: the peninsula of

Margaritis, which closes the deep bay of Mármaro on its east side is visibly scarred with signs of the ancient extraction of a compact, opaque and fine-grained, grey-black stone, similar to the better known North African '*nero antico*' and occurring sometimes with the browner tonality of '*bigio morato*'. From the southeastern corner of the bay, a road (*unsigned turning after 1km, just before bridge*) leads into the tranquil, wooded northeastern promontory of the island and up to the panoramic point of **Megali Vigla**, 260m above the sea (6km detour), looking over Oinousses and the Karaburnu peninsula into Turkey. Beyond the church of **Aghia Irini**, the track descends to a beautiful stretch of coast comprising a series of pebble coves, rocks promontories and clear water, which is good for bathing. Surface finds have suggested that the southernmost cove, **Vroulídia Bay** (5km), was used as a harbour in Hellenistic and Roman times.

AROUND MOUNT PELINNAION

Four and a half kilometres northwest from Mármaro is **Nagos**—whose name is a corruption of *naos*, 'a temple', the 4th century BC remains of which were found during excavations (now covered) in the vicinity of the spring, to the west side of the village. The steep, densely treed slope of the mountain dropping down to the sea, run through by the waterfalls of a torrent, marks a dramatic change in landscape, announcing what is to come to the west of here. As the road rises into wilder and steeper hills, the pines give way to deciduous forest, where the abundant water, humidity and tree-cover are home to a rich **flora**. The yellow **fritillary**, *Fritillaria pelinaea*, whose petals have a greenish tinge towards the stem, grows here (and nowhere else in the world) in the area of the villages of **Amádes** and **Víki**, and higher up the mountain slopes beneath the pine and maple trees. In the autumn, several varieties of the crocus-like *Sternbergia* are a common and beautiful sight. In the air above, there are always birds of prey—short-toed eagles, long-legged buzzards, and occasionally some particularly unusual species, such as the **Levantine sparrowhawk**, distinguishable by its pronounced dark wingtips on the pale under-side of the wings. The ravines below are full of nightingale song in the spring. The villages are isolated, densely-packed clusters of stone houses—often small towers, of the kind noted at Anávatos—built around springs and churches marked with stands of plane-trees in their central squares.

The road turns south at **Kambiá** (47km from Chora), a village famous for its production (and festivals) of cherries: to the north, on precipitous rock-stacks in the ravine below, are the ruined **castle of Oria** and the precariously perched church of the **Panaghia**; to the west are hillsides, traced and retraced with stone walls defining an extraordinary variety of shapes across the barren rocky terrain; to the south (2.5km) the watershed is marked by the remains of a mediaeval watchtower, directly east of the **peak of Mount Pelinnaion**, which rises to a craggy 1,297m above. The summit is best reached by the safer route from Víki, which is marked and takes about two and a half hours each way; otherwise there is a slightly longer and shadeless route up from **Spartounda** (5km south of Kambiá). The upper slopes of the summit are home to the beautiful mauve-blue, alpine squill, *Cilla bifolia*, and the elusive *Campanula cymbalaria*.

From Spartoúnda, there are expansive views of the west of the island and across the water to Psará. The surrounding landscape has re-grown with scrub vegetation after repeated fires: only the hardiest **pine-trees** have survived and, in consequence, have grown into solitary and massive, sculpted forms, memorials to the forests that until recently clad these slopes. At 16km from Kambiá, and 2km north of the junction with the main east/west road from Vrontados to Volissos, a turning branches off the road to the west and drops down (0.5km) to the monastery of Aghios Ioannis Prodromos, known as *Moni Moundón,

which sits on an eminence just above the village of Dievchá. For the combination of its position with stunning
views (especially at sunset), its atmospheric ruined buildings, and its unusual cycles of wall-paintings, this is one
of the most interesting monasteries in northern Chios.
(*Outer buildings always open, though now undergoing restoration. Catholicon closed; key has to be obtained from the
custodian in the village of Dievchá. T. 22740 22011*). Originally a late 15th century foundation, the monastery was
enlarged and re-established in 1574 by a certain Iakovos
Langadiotis, after which it acquired considerable importance on the island functioning as a monastic retreat and
school for the Chiot aristocracy: it possessed a large and
significant library. Although devastated in 1822, it was restored and re-decorated only to be abandoned finally a
century later. Inside, the ruined buildings line both sides
of a paved pathway which leads from the grandly **domed
entrance** built in the 16th century, to a similar, roofed
loggia in front of the west door of the *catholicon*.

Archival material shows that there were no fewer than three
campaigns of paintings in the *catholicon* in the 17th and
18th centuries, the sum of which was lost in the damage
wrought in 1822: the present paintings date from 1849, with
restorations carried out after the earthquake of 1881. They

figure many traditional images of the icon-painter's gamut, treated with the attractive *naïveté* of 'folk art'. A good example is the *Ladder to Heaven*, in which a huddle of robed monks, encouraged by St Michael, leave the security of the cloister to attempt the precarious ladder that ascends to Heaven, while demons attempt to derail their endeavours. On the south wall is a more idiosyncratic scene—*The Life of the True Monk*, in which the crucified monk is flanked by Hell to one side and by the worlds of temptation and death to the other.

THE LIMESTONE PLATEAU OF MOUNT AIPOS: PITIOS & RIMOKASTRO

Two kilometres south of Moni Moundon the road rejoins the main east/west road from Vrontados to Volissos: 7km further to the east through scattered pine forests, in the direction of Chora, a branch road to left leads off to Pitiós (3.6km).

Mount Pelinnaíon is a grand massif with conspicuous peaks, while Mount Aípos, to its south, is quite different in character—a wide, shadeless, undulating mountain plateau of seemingly waterless rock. In a cleft between the two, sits the once remote settlement of **Pitiós**. A small area of cultivable land surrounds the village—a patchwork of fertile fields on the side of Mount Pelinnaíon, and barren on the side of Mount Aípos. A long but tendentious local tradition links the village with Homer; until not long ago, visitors were shown the 'house where the poet was born'. The village is dominated by its 13th century **fort**—a curious military building shaped in plan like a half-melon, with a curved castellated front to the north and a flat side to the south: the unusual shape is not dictated by the space available on the rock outcrop, but may arise from modifications made when a pre-existing, four-square Byzantine fort was reinforced by the Genoese, using more up-to-date military architecture.

Returning to the main road once again, and continuing east towards Chora, a landscape of frightening austerity unfolds. At the summit, after 7.1km, a rough track leads back (1.5km) to the north across the rock plateau to **Rimókastro**. On a shallow rise, with commanding views across to Oinousses, are the camouflaged remains of collapsed stone walls covering a large area; in the midst of this desolate scene is an outbreak of clearly cut and finished, rectangular blocks, belonging to an ancient, late-**Classical** or **Hellenistic building**, originally constructed in isodomic masonry, and apparently divided into three rooms. The threshold of the east door is carefully cut with **escape channels** for rainwater at the ends of the sill. The bleak and waterless rock around invites speculation as to the purpose of such a building. An absence of votive objects and a mass of potsherds of domestic items, suggests that this was a large **farmstead** (perhaps for the raising of a particularly tough and tenacious breed of livestock?) which may well have doubled up, as so often in the Hellenistic world, as a fortified look-out post.

From the summit beside the turning for Rimókastro, the road descends slowly, towards the precipitous edge of the plateau of Mount Aípos. Seven kilometres short of Chios town, it reaches a belvedere with a sudden and ***magnificent panorama** of Vrontados and Chios far below, and the mountains of Turkey stretching beyond. The descent is dramatic thereafter. The ingeniously constructed **retaining walls of the modern road** have been made from using the flattened flagstones from the paved surface of the old road, whose route the modern road closely follows down a precipitous descent of over three hundred metres in altitude.

EPILOGUE
THE MASSACRE OF CHIOS, 1822

Nicholas I of Russia was himself sick and fevered when he reputedly referred to the Ottoman Empire as the 'sick man of Europe'. As the Persians, the Romans, the Byzantines, the French, the British, all know, the terminal loss of power, territory and influence for any great empire is a traumatic business. The greater the empire, the more profound the trauma; and the Ottoman Empire was among the greatest in history. Panic, remorse, and often violent over-reaction are the unpredictable, yet inevitable, accompaniments that wait on the long retreat of a declining power, as they do on a wounded animal. The terrible events of April 1822 in Chios, which should never be diminished in horror by explanation, need nonetheless to be seen in the widest context if they are adequately to be accounted for. Chios was dealt a difficult hand by events, and it became in 1822 one of the unfortunate 'sacrificial victms' of history. Greece was alight with the fever of insurrection at the time; much of Europe's intellectual elite, fired by the antiquarian heroism embodied by Byron, and moved more generally by an ancient disdain and fear of Islam, supported its cause. The Greek insurrection was sometimes heroic, and sometimes violent and genocidal itself. The year before the massacre in Chios took place, some 15,000 Turkish men and women had been slaughtered in southern Greece in a fever of ethnic cleansing. 'Not a Turk shall remain in the Morea,' was a common slogan. Sir Charles Eliot, British diplomat and distinguished scholar of Buddhism, writing in his book *Turkey in Europe* published in London in 1900, made reference to such events 'not', he said, 'from a desire to prove that Turks and Greeks are all much of a muchness, but [to show] that it is important to realize that the Turks really have cause to fear Christians.' Earlier, in the introduction to the book, he had observed: 'the ordinary Turk is an honest, good-humoured soul, kind to children and animals, and very patient; but when the fighting spirit comes on him, he ... slays, burns and ravages without mercy or discrimination'. Why did that fighting spirit come upon the Turks in Chios, which historically had had such close ties with Istanbul?

Precisely because of those close ties—commercial,

political and even perhaps of mutual respect—Chios was slow to embrace outright the cause of the Greek Revolution. As one of the richest trading centres in the eastern Mediterranean, it was unsure whether it should hazard and give up a long tradition of accommodation and commercial cooperation with the Ottoman Empire which had brought the island substantial autonomy, in exchange for the unknown benefits of the administration of a new Greek State. The leaders of the island were merchants and scholars, not military revolutionaries. They hesitated—something which must have appeared to the firebrands of the movement like disaffection with the cause of Greek Independence. As a result, Samos, which was a relatively poor island at that time and had much less to lose, sent an expeditionary force under Lycourgos Logothetis in March 1822 to incite the Chiots to join the revolution, because their participation was considered vital to the cause. Logothetis landed at Karfás, but his mission soon lost its strategic objective and was diverted into what became a frustrated and uncontrolled plundering of the riches of a neighbouring island. When news of his arrival on Chios reached Istanbul, the possibility of losing Chios—the most valuable of the Ottoman possessions in the Aegean—first began to seem a reality.

The Istanbul to which the news came, was itself in a moment of weakness. Sultan Mahmud II, who had come to the throne as a child in 1808, was intent on wide-reaching reforms, first and foremost in the army where the spectre of mutiny haunted the historic corps of the Janissaries. The Janissaries were ultimately disbanded in 1826; but in 1822 they, and with them the defences of the Ottoman Empire, were clearly in disarray. In moments of weakness, great powers react unpredictably. Fearing that the loss of important Chios might provoke a wider 'domino' collapse, Mahmud ordered the execution of hostages which had been taken as a precautionary measure in both Chios and from its community in Istanbul. He dispatched his admiral, Kara Ali Pasha, with a fleet of ships and crack troops to the island where they arrived on 11 April. The orders were to retake Chios, and to kill men over the age of 12 and women over the age of 40. The city was first bombarded; then, with the landing of more troops from Smyrna, a systematic destruction of life and property began. About 2,000 people, predominantly women and children, who took refuge at Nea Moni, were killed or burnt alive when the monastery was torched by Turkish troops. With the implacable and merciless 'fighting spirit' intimated by Charles Eliot, the Turks pushed far into the island, destroying and capturing entire communities such as Avgónyma and Anávatos. After Constantine Kanaris's destruction of the Turkish flagship together with its admiral, Kara Ali Pasha, on 18 June, another bout of Turkish reprisals began; but by then there was little left to destroy and little population on which to exact revenge. Estimates vary; but between 20–25,000 people were killed on Chios, and a further 40–45,000 young men, women and children, were captured and deported into slavery, confinement or destitution.

The scale of these reprisals sent shockwaves through the chanceries of Europe and into the world of those intellectuals and artists who, like Byron and Victor Hugo, had identified with the Greek cause. Eugène Delacroix—only 24 years old at the time of the events—immortalised them in his grand and tragic painting, *Le Massacre de Scio*, which was exhibited in the Grand Salon in Paris less than two years later. The painting is not a historical picture of what happened; the figures are arrayed across the foreground in a deliberate recollection of poses from ancient Greek reliefs, as if to underscore the terrible immanence and repetition of violence throughout the history of the 'civilised world'.

How was Chios to continue after this? An island is like a person: individual and complete. It can thrive on its own, but it can also collapse on its own; it does not have the seamless contact with a greater whole which a mainland city or region has, and which can help it to absorb the blows of destiny. The loss of a large proportion of its population—amongst them nearly all of those who managed and directed its affairs and economy—and the destruction of dwellings and infrastructure in one blow, was enough to cause total collapse in a circumscribed community such as Chios was in the 19th century. Massacres have happened countless times before and since in history, and continue to happen today in different places; but in an island the effect of such a catastrophe is more acute precisely because of its physical isolation. In 1822 Chios was a prosperous, sophisticated and tightly-knit community that had been trading and shipping in Europe and Western Asia for centuries: after the mayhem of the massacres, its spirit was simply broken. The few who survived had fled and were to settle permanently elsewhere; the critical mass, that makes a community and its culture, and markets function, was no longer there. And what little could be salvaged was anyway destroyed 59 years later in the devastating earthquake of 1881. Chios was not like a mainland city, where the incessant flow and movement of people in and out could help it easily reconstitute after these disasters. A long chapter of the island's history ended in 1822. It is a busy and prospering place today, of course; but that is because it is fundamentally a different place.

PRACTICAL INFORMATION

821 00/02 & 822 00 Chios: area 841 sq. km; perimeter 213km; resident population 51,060; max. altitude 1,297m. **Port Authority**: T. 22710 44433. **Travel and information**: Municipal Tourist Office, T. 22710 44389, www.chiosonline.gr

ACCESS

By air: Domestic flights from Athens, three times daily with *Olympic Air* and twice daily with *Aegean Airlines*, serve Chios throughout the year. Five days a week there are Olympic Air connections with Thessaloniki, including a twice weekly local, Eastern Aegean route, from Thessaloniki to Rhodes, via Lemnos, Mytilini and (once a week only) Samos. The airport is 3km from the centre of Chios town.

By boat: The principal route—Piraeus, Chios, Mytilini—is served by **Hellenic Seaways**, with a daily 12.30 departure from Piraeus, arriving Chios at 7pm, continuing to Mytilini, and returning to Piraeus overnight. **NEL Lines** run three times weekly along the route from/to Samos to the south, and Mytilini, Lemnos, and Kavala, to the north. Smaller ferry-boats connect Chios with Psará (5 times weekly), and Oinousses (6 times weekly). Crossings to Turkey (Çeşme) run almost daily during the summer season (Easter–mid-October); thereafter much more infrequently.

LODGING

A number of the nicest places to stay on Chios are in Kampos, to the south of the main town, in the elegant stone villas which are so characteristic of the area. Two, that are close to one another, and run by different members of the same family, are particularly recommended: *Perivoli (*Argenti Street, T. 22710 31513, fax 32042, www.perivolihotel. gr*), and *Perleas (*Vitiadou Street, T. 22710 32217, fax 32364, www.perleas.gr*). Both offer simple accommodation and attentive hospitality, moderately priced, in elegant villas with gardens. Although signposted, neither is easy to find: if you call ahead, you will be piloted, or collected. There is public transport to this area, but a rental vehicle is advised. In the centre of town, at the south end of the port, is the **Hotel Kyma** in a stone-built mansion looking onto the sea (*T. 22710 44500, fax 44600, email: kyma@chi. forthnet.gr*); the antiquity of the plumbing and bedroom furniture are more than compensated for by the friendliness and attentive hospitality of the owners and by the charm of the building. A different experience is offered by

Spilia Xenonas at Kardámyla above the northeast coast, 23km from the port (*T. 22720 22933, fax 22823, www. spilia-chios.gr*). This is a group of small, carefully restored, characteristic, stone cottages at the top of the village, with views towards the sea in the distance: a good homemade breakfast is provided. Wooden signposts guide you up to the cottages on steep stone paths through the village; any car will need to be left some distance below.

EATING

Delightful, welcoming and with fresh, imaginative dishes and good *bourekakia* (lightly filled and fried filo-pastry rolls), is the (recently much enlarged) taverna, **Roussikó**, in Thymianá (just east of the main church in the village). In the main town of Chios: both '**Byzantinio**' and '**Elleniki Kouzina**', on opposite sides of the crossing of Ralli and Roïdou Streets between the port and the public gardens, are favoured by locals for their clean environment, inexpensive home-cooking and well-prepared, worka-day food; no frills and no atmosphere, just simple food. **Iakovou** (evenings only), on Aghios Giorgios Street in the Kastro, has more atmosphere and offers a number of Asia Minor dishes. Around the island: **Lefteris** at Pandoukiós (just south of Langada on the northeast coast), **Tria Adelphia** on Lithí Beach (central west Chios) and the taverna, **Limani Meston** in

Liménas (southwest Chios), all offer excellent, fresh fish-dishes in pleasant settings by the shore; while **Markellos** at Pitiós is well-known for meat and vegetable dishes of local cuisine; and **Pheragides** offers mezes in the delightful setting of a plane-shaded plateia at Kardámyla in northeastern Chios.

The cliffs and rocky coasts of Chios are home to an aromatic **samphire** ('*kritamo*') which is a distinctive element of its salads—always worth asking for, if it has not already been included in the mixture. Chios also has a tradition of excellence in oriental pastries; the quality of the *baklava* and other sweets made by the **Amandier Patisserie** in Livanou Street (south side of port) is worthy of any Ottoman pastry-chef.

FURTHER READING

For social history of the important families of Chios and for the events of 1821/2 the following site contains much valuable information: www.christopherlong.co.uk/pub/chiosinfo.html

OINOUSSES

In 2004, an 80-foot mid-4th century BC cargo-vessel, carrying around 400 *amphorae* of wine, was found underwater, wrecked in the channel between Chios and Oinousses; and in the same year a Roman shipwreck with similar cargo was identified off the west of Chios. These are neither the first nor the last of many such submarine finds: each new season, it seems, brings more evidence of the formidable quantity of wine traded through these waters in Antiquity. The name Oinousses, or Ancient *Oinousa*, means 'rich in wine'. That richness could have been in the production, but was more probably in the trading, of wine. The nine or ten islands that comprise the archipelago of Oinousses are not naturally rich in any produce; their economic potential lies solely in their strategic position as stepping-stones between Asia and Chios—proximity to the rich markets of Chios, Ephesus and Smyrna (Izmir), and a well-protected harbour. Without boats, and wine to trade, the islands would have been nothing. It is a parable of the indomitable Hellenic spirit—the Greek '*emporiko pnevma*' or 'commercial enterprise'—that these islands, which are about as productive as Coll or Tiree in the Hebrides, should have given rise to several of the wealthiest families in Europe, principally ship-brokers, who have dominated the international world of commercial navigation. Greek families still control, between them, the largest merchant navy in the world, and perhaps as many as a third of those families hail from these obscure islands in the channel between Turkey and Greece. Since earliest times boats have signified freedom and enterprise for the Greeks. Greek civilisation is predicated on them. And on the exchange of goods and ideas which they promote. On Oinousses the choices for survival were simple: either boats or goat-herding.

The visitor who comes expecting a sophisticated and well provided-for island in consequence of this immense wealth will be disappointed. There are statues of shipping grandees; some smart villas; a beautifully appointed Nautical Museum; a modern football stadium (somewhat out of proportion to its setting and the island's size); and a state-of-the-art nunnery which does not encourage visitors. But, as ways of repatriating wealth from the prestigious families to the community, the projects visible on Oinousses are all slightly self-serving: some respectable street paving, a café or two, and a shop might have helped more to re-animate the declining community, and would have cost far less. The contrast with Andros and Syros (whose wealth also derives from important shipping families) is marked, in this respect. Oinousses still feels like a forgotten frontier. Its peacefulness, the wide views into Turkey and to Chios afforded by walks over its hills, and the dense and unusually varied vegetation of its *garrigue*, are its greatest attractions.

HISTORY

Evidence of the mercantile potential of these islands can be inferred from a reference in Herodotus (*Hist.* I. 165): after the abandonment of their besieged city during the Ionian revolt, the people of Phocaea sailed to Chios and asked the Chians if they could purchase the islands of *Oinousa* and settle there; Chios refused, fearing that the islands 'might be made into a new centre of commerce to the exclusion of their own'. The Phocaeans were renowned seafarers and traders, and would not presumably have made such an offer had they not seen the island's hidden trading potential. Thereafter the islands are, in effect, an extension of Chian territory and follow the history of their large and important neighbour. In the Middle Ages the islands were probably abandoned; repopulation from Kardámyla began in the 18th century. At the time of the 1822 massacre on Chios, the inhabitants fled to Syros, then the Aegean centre for Greek shipping. Within 40 years of returning to the island five years later, Oinoussaian families between them owned almost thirty ships, plying routes through the Mediterranean and Black Sea.

The emergence in the 19th century of three important

families or 'clans', in particular, on the island—the Hadji-pateras, Lemos and Lyras families—and their formation of a consortium was the beginning of the story of long-distance, international shipping for Oinousses. In 1905 they purchased their first steamer, the 3,500 ton, *Marietta Rallis*. With characteristic resilience, after substantial losses in the Second World War, the group took advantage of the possibility to purchase 'Liberty Ships' (a standardised and rapidly built cargo ship of British design, which was produced in large numbers by American shipyards during the war) from the US government, and contracted a number of new cargo ships from shipyards in Japan and Yugoslavia. In the 1950s the same group founded 'Orient Mid-East Lines', which ran liner services between the USA, the Mediterranean and Far East. The Lemos family holding of shipping is by most measures the largest private holding in Greece, and one of the largest in the world. In 1962 the Pateras family built, and richly endowed, the nunnery of the *Evangelismos*, at the west end of the island, in memory of a daughter of the family, Irini, who died at 20 and is considered by some a candidate for sanctification: the abbess of the convent is her mother.

AIGNOUSA

The ferry docks at the harbour of **Aignousa**: the port is formed by a protective chain of islets to west and south, which are crowned with churches. One islet, which has a family villa to the north end, is clearly marked 'Pateròniso' ('Pateras island'), in case there should be any doubt as to its ownership. The main waterfront is remarkable for a Greek island in its lack of the customary buzz of cafés and shops; out of season, there are none. It is punctuated by several bronze statues of members of the prominent Pateras and Lemos families, as well as more symbolic memorials—to the 'Unknown Sailor', the *Mother of Oinoussaians* (1979), and the *Mermaid of the Port*.

In the centre of the promenade is the recently renovated **Maritime Museum** (*generally open mornings in high season only*).

This is a remarkable collection of models, cannon, nautical instruments and machinery, and a number of fine painted **figureheads**. There are also two cases of antiquities from Cyprus, and armaments of the 18th and 19th centuries.

An important section of the museum is the Antonis Lemos collection of over 30 **models of ships**, executed with great craftsmanship by French prisoners of war during the Napoleonic Wars: many of the models are of battleships used in the conflicts between the French and British. The prisoners were taken in the period between 1793 and 1815, and were interned at Portsmouth: while in captivity they supplemented their meagre rations with this activity—at first using chicken and fish bones from the kitchens, and then, as their skills became evident, adding other materials which were provided for them, such as the cotton for the rigging. The models are not always accurate, but are intricately and finely constructed.

The other strength of the museum is the collection of more than twenty attractive **watercolours** by the successful and popular artist of ships and marine subjects, **Aristides Glykas** (1870–1940), who was a native of Chios. His intimate knowledge of ships came from his having been a mariner. His art marks the passage of taste from the world of the international professional painter of ships' portraits to that of the local Greek, 'folk' portraitists. The pictures have a freshness and simplicity. They were largely done on commission, and are mostly static images; but, occasionally there are dramatic scenes such as that of the *Torpedoing of the Agios Georgios in 1917* by a German submarine. Glykas used the simplest materials: glue from almonds or from fishbones for the priming of his cardboard supports and as a distemper for the simple colours. He generally used an Indian ink for the blue. Latterly he began to work with oils.

At the western end of the waterfront promenade is the *Navtiko Gymnasio*, or Academy of Commercial Navigation—the only non-military, nautical boarding school in Greece. From this point there is a good general view back over the Chora, which spreads attractively to one side of a cavea-shaped hollow in the hills.

The **Chora** is surprisingly large, and spreads substantially to the east onto the slopes of the next valley. The **original settlement**, founded in the mid-18th century in times of insecurity from piracy, lay higher up the hillside, 2km to the northeast, just below the ridge of the island. Only the ruins of stone habitations remain. The modern settlement is grouped around the large **church of Aghios Nikolaos**, an early 20th century building, lavishly decorated inside and well endowed with icons; the church functions as the 'centre', since there is curiously no *plateia*—no real heart to the town. On the climb up from the port you pass a number of fine neoclassical buildings—many abandoned—with window frames and carved architectural details in stone. On the hill to the west is the community's **cemetery**—of interest for the names of the shipping families represented. There are a number of marble mausolea of different branches of the Lemos and Pateras families; but the difference in artistic quality between these and the much finer memorials in the cemeteries in Syros and Andros is marked.

AROUND THE ISLAND

The coastal road, which leaves from beside the cemetery, passes through an area scattered with houses and signs of abandoned cultivation. The slopes of the hills facing the sea here are covered with a **rich maquis** of arbutus, rosemary, thyme, saxifrage, broom, euphorbia and cistus, whose colours, density and fragrance are greater because so little disturbed.

After 30 minutes (3.5km) the road rises steeply towards the north affording good views of northern Chios. At the top of the rise, the **convent of the Annunciation of the Virgin** (*Evangelismós tis Theotókou*) comes partially into view, sunk in a fold in the hills amongst pine and fir trees. The nunnery, for all its wealth, is not large or particularly showy: it is just meticulously constructed from the best materials and deliberately hidden behind manicured hedges of cypress and jasmine. Above it on the crest of the hill is a landmark cross, with the **church of the Análipsi** (the Ascension) just beyond; below it, nearer to the shore,

are the gardens which supply the religious community.
Men are not permitted entry to the convent: the author
therefore is at a disadvantage in describing the interior.

> The convent was built in 1962 at the wish of Katingo Pateras,
> grieving mother of a daughter of 20, Irini, who, after a life
> of genuine but precocious piety, died of cancer. Her father,
> Panagos Pateras, had contracted Hodgkin's disease; it is said
> that Irini prayed that the disease be taken from her father
> and visited on her instead. The father improved or at least
> went into remission; the daughter fell ill; and after taking
> vows as a nun, she died in 1959. Three years later her body
> was exhumed and it was discovered that the corpse had not
> decayed, but rather had been preserved and desiccated by
> burial. Many—first and foremost, Katingo Pateras—saw this
> apparent miracle as a sign of her sainthood. The body of
> Irini is now kept in a glass coffin inside the convent built by
> her mother, who elected to become the community's Abess.
> Panagos Pateras died in 1965.

The upper road which runs back east along the ridge of
the hills, skirts the island's summit, **Voutyro** (182m), with
views towards the mainland of Turkey. A little beyond,
after a thick stand of pines, are the remains of a small settlement in a hollow; this safer, more hidden site, is all that

remains of the **earlier settlement** on the island, before the development of the modern port-town of Aignousa. To the east the **panorama** is delightful, over rolling hills which, in the middle distance, alternate with water towards the extremity of the archipelago, and finally blend seamlessly with the hills of the Karaburnu promontory and the bay of Ancient *Erythraia*. There are many sheltered inlets and little habitation in this gentler half of the island.

PRACTICAL INFORMATION

82 101 Oinousses: area 14 sq. km; perimeter 35km; resident population 686; max. altitude 182 m. **Port Authority:** Oinousses, T. 22710 55394; Chios, T. 22710 44433.

The archipelago consists of about 10 islands: Oinousses is the largest and the only one continuously to be inhabited; Panaghia (or Pasas), Vatos, Pontikoniso, Gaidouroniso (or Gavathi), Archontoniso, lie to the east; Aghios Panteleimon and Pateroniso, lie just outside the harbour; and the two small islets referred to as the 'Prasonisi', lie to the west.

ACCESS

The local ferry boat from Chios, *Oinoussai III* (T. 22710 25074), runs daily except Tues, leaving Oinousses for Chios early in the morning, and returning after lunch. Crossing time: 1hr. Two small water-taxis ply the shorter route between Oinousses and Langada (NE Chios) at all hours, on demand (T. 6944 168 104).

FURTHER READING

One chapter of *Hellas* (Collins, London, 1987) by Nicholas Gage is devoted to the shipping families of Oinousses—more entertaining, than strictly accurate.

LODGING

Lodging is limited to the **Thalassoporos Hotel** (*T. 22720 55745*) where the accommodation is basic, but the owners are particularly friendly.

EATING

Eating is also very limited. The only fully-fledged taverna is the pleasant enough **Taverna Pateròniso**, set back a little way from the harbour front; up in the town are a couple of shops that double as small eateries. The fare is basic at them all, and there is little to choose between them.

PSARA

A water-colour by Nikolaos Koutsodontis in the Benaki Museum in Athens, entitled *The Burning of Psará in June 1824*, shows the whole island encircled by the innumerable ships of a swarming Ottoman Navy, while Turkish soldiers who have landed set fires alight across its length and breadth. Although somewhat artless as a painting, it is a chilling reminder of the magnitude of the Ottoman show of force on that occasion. Exactly two years after the Massacre at Chios, it fell to this small island to suffer

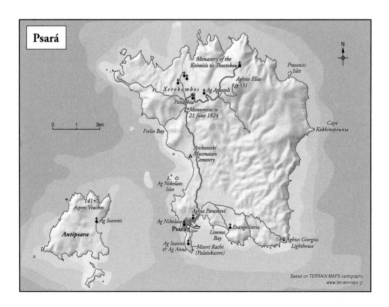

once again the brunt of Turkish reprisals for its pugna-
cious naval resistance to colonial rule during the Greek
War of Independence. On this occasion virtually nothing was spared. The island—formerly prosperous and
outward-looking—was laid waste, and has never properly
recovered.

The poverty of its land, with not even vines enough
to make the customary libations to Dionysos, was noted
in Antiquity. It is little wonder that the islanders turned
to the sea therefore and became talented mariners—famous for their skill at combating pirates—and operating
a substantial commercial navy in the 18th and early 19th
centuries. Those who escaped the reprisals of 1824 settled
in Syros, in an area of the city known to this day as 'Psari-
aná': they went on once again to become a vital element
in the lucrative shipping industry of the island, continuing their age-old tradition as expert seamen.

The names—'Psará', meaning 'the greys' or 'grizzled
things'; 'Mavri Rachi' ('black ridge') for the acropolis-like
rock that dominates the port—are eloquent of the island's
character. Arrival at Psará is always sombre: the island has
a beautiful and sculpted profile, but its rock is as barren
and dark as its story is tragic. Today, fewer than 500 souls
inhabit what remains of the once elegant main town. This
is an island where visitors are not that often seen, nor is

being a visitor here particularly easy. Accommodation is limited and no public transportation exists on the island. It has two interesting, historic sites: the important Mycenaean settlement at Archontikí and the fine monastery of the Dormition, at the northern extremity of the island. But both are hard to get access to: a perimeter fence at Archontikí, constructed with European Union funds, now excludes the visitor and there is no official news of the site being open. The monastery is uninhabited and kept locked: its interior can only be visited together with the island's elderly priest and with some arranged means to transport him there.

Together with Aghios Efstratios, Psará remains among the remotest of Aegean destinations, and much of its appeal lies in the peace and tranquillity that fact affords. The island is open and spacious like the remotest Hebrides, and its strands—though grey and shadeless—are tranquil. Psará is a place of retreat for quiet contemplation of the strange vicissitudes of history.

HISTORY

Because of its strategic position at the edge of open waters on the trade routes leading from the south west Aegean towards the Black Sea and Asia Minor coasts, Psará had a flourishing Mycenaean settlement in the 14th and 13th centuries BC. The site, which lies along the island's western shore at Lákka, has yielded almost 50 cist graves with a wealth of grave-gifts, both of metal and pottery.

The first written reference to the island is in Book III of the *Odyssey*, where its name is given by Nestor as '*Psyria*'. Strabo mentions its good harbour, and Demosthenes refers to the island in connection with the strong winds that hinder navigation in its waters—a fact no less true today. Excavations have revealed Hellenistic settlement close by the site of the present town at Mavri Rachi, and a Roman presence both at Xerókambos in the north of the island and in the Limnos Bay area on the south coast.

In the First Russo-Turkish war of 1768–74 Psariot ships harried the Turkish fleet but escaped reprisals because the Ottoman commander was prevented from landing by bad weather. The island's fleet subsequently achieved protection and prosperity by sailing under the Russian flag after the termination of hostilities with the Treaty of

Küçük Kaynarca (1774) between Catherine the Great and Sultan Abdul Hamid I. Psará was the birthplace of Ioannis Varvakis (1745–1825), Nikolis Apostolis (1770–1827), Constantine Kanaris (?1793–1877), and many other noted sailors. At the beginning of the war of Greek Independence in 1821 the island was among the first to revolt, proceeding to cause the Turkish fleet particular annoyance. Under the command of Nikolis Apostolis, Psará formed, together with Hydra and Spetses, the 'Three Island Fleet' which was to play such an important role in the uprising. Refugees began to arrive from Chios, Lesbos and Smyrna, swelling the population to perhaps as much as 20,000. In 1823 the Psariot fleet raided the coast of Asia Minor: in revenge, the Turks under their Egyptian commander, Hosref Pasha, attacked the island from Mytilene in May 1824, surrounding it with a force of 140 ships and finally storming it in June with 14,000 Janissaries. The islanders blew up their own powder magazines at Fteltó and at Mavri Rachi, and only 3,000 souls escaped the subsequent massacre. Ruined houses, a couple of simple white memorials, and a famous six-line epigram by Dionysios Solomos bear witness to the event. The few survivors fled to Syros and to Monemvasia, and later founded 'Nea Psará' (at Eretria) on Euboea. In spite of special electoral privileges given to the island in 1844 and Franco-Greek social and cultural projects initiated in the 1980s, the island has never truly recovered momentum.

FROM THE PORT TO
MONI KOIMISEOS THEOTOKOU

The large sheltered bay of Psará on the southwest corner of the island is formed of two wide sweeps, protected to the south by the steep and looming **rock of Mávri Ráchi** or 'Palaiokastro', formerly the acropolis of Ancient *Psyra* in historic times: traces of a Hellenistic settlement (3rd to 1st centuries BC) have been uncovered by archaeologists on the north slope, with the cemetery occupying the lowest reaches. Today the summit of the ridge is gained by means of a stepped, stone path which leads up to the church of **Aghia Anna and Aghios Ioannis**, standing on a terrace at the top. The tumbled remains of walls can be seen here, running south along the ridge; but they are too ruined and subject to subsequent modification to bear any recognisable ancient character. Some of the blocks in the north corner of the west front of Aghia Anna, however, may be antique; above, the façade is decorated with immured tiles and ceramic dishes. A simple monument to the south of the church records the hopeless resistance here of the locals against the punitive Turkish invasion of 1824 (*see 'History' above*). There are fine **views** towards Chios to the east; and to Andros and Euboea, visible on the horizon to the southwest and west respectively, when conditions are clear. Immediately west, in the foreground, is the pleasing form of the island of Antípsara—uninhabited by humans and for that reason a favoured nesting site for the shearwaters and shags which frequent the open waters to the west.

The town spreads across the isthmus which joins Mávri Ráchi to the island and over the low saddle behind the port, rising to a ridge crowned by the conspicuously tall, white structure of the mid 19th century church of **Aghios Nikolaos**, built on the site of an 18th century predecessor which was destroyed in the Turkish invasion. The fine flight of **marble stairs** which lead up to it from the town, belonged to the earlier building. Ceramic fragments and dishes are immured high up on its east wall. The church has an unusually tall and luminous interior: there are views to Antípsara and into the sunset from the esplanade in front.

Of greater interest is the small church hidden in a garden under a scarp below the eastern terrace of Aghios

Nikolaos. The church, which dates from 1710, has two dedications—to the **Taxiarchis** and to **Aghios Spyridon**—and two aisles separated by columns. The roof is attractively tiled with large schist slabs in the manner of churches in the Sporades. This building was already over 80 years old when **Constantine Kanaris**, the island's preeminent hero, was born in a house a short distance to its northeast. The birthplace is marked by a small memorial garden, with a statue bust of the great admiral; the house itself was destroyed in 1824. The town is scattered with several similar memorials to other contemporary naval heroes born on Psará: Dimitris Papanikolaos (south harbour mole); Kanaris again (main square); Nikolis Apostolis (northeast battery). Papanikolaos was the first naval captain to employ (Eresos, 27 May 1821) a 'fire-ship' to destroy an enemy vessel—a technique that was to prove immensely effective in the struggle against the Ottoman navy in the subsequent months.

Constantine Kanaris was born into a prominent family on the island in 1793 or 1795. He was a deft and courageous captain. His career began with his most symbolic achievement, when, during the night of June 6/7th 1822 as the Turkish command was celebrating the destruction of Chios on board their flagship anchored off shore, he approached unnoticed with a fire-tender and exploded it, killing the Turkish admiral, Kara Ali Paşa, his officers and all the men on board. Kanaris went on to score important naval victories at Trikeri (1823), Samos and Tenedos (1824), and at Alexandria (1825). He later served six separate terms as Prime Minister of Greece between 1844 and 1877, both before and after the bloodless revolution which deposed King Otho of Greece in 1862, in which he played an important role. He died, a national hero in 1877.

The centre of the town circles around a low rise dominated by the domed church of the **Metamorphosis** (the Transfiguration) dating from 1865—similarly tall and luminous in design to Aghios Nikolaos, and with an attractively carved marble frame to the south door. A walk through the neighbouring streets, which connect a myriad of tiny squares, reveals an interesting **variety of architecture**, even though one in three buildings is a ruin. Of the buildings which remain from before the Turkish destruction, the most interesting examples are on the rise of the northeast battery which separates the two bays of the port. Here, two buildings dating from the first two decades of the 19th century, are in a Levantine style of architecture typical of Chios—flat-roofed, built of two colours of stone and with small-framed windows in white marble. On the chamfered corner of one is an Ottoman decorative plaque in marble with pomegranate-design. Further to the north is a new rectangular building, recreated successfully in the same style and a similar variety of colours of stone: this is destined to become the Nautical Museum of Psará, but currently has no exhibits. In its forecourt (west side) lies an **ancient marble slab**, curiously carved with two partly legible, parallel inscriptions of different epochs mentioning a dedication made to Apollo (right), and referring to a comic actor from Smyrna (left). Just beyond, at the eastern edge of the settlement, is the town's oldest church—**Aghia Paraskevi**—dating from the late 17th century and now surrounded by the island's cemetery.

From the main town two excursions can be made by starting from the road which heads east from the church of Aghia Paraskevi. The first, by continuing *east*, leads to the remote bay and lighthouse of Aghios Giorgios (1hr by foot), or by a southern branch track to the beach at **Limnos Bay** (25 mins). Potsherds of the Roman period have been found all along this first stretch of the coast to the east. The bay is backed by one of only two small alluvial areas on the island that lend themselves to any kind of cultivation: elsewhere the island is of a barren and waterless, dark rock, alleviated by occasional, curious veins or excrescences of gleaming white gypsum.

By taking the *north* branch 500m beyond Aghia Paraskevi, you climb over a ridge and after passing a wind
farm drop down into the bay of Lákka. At the northern
end of the bay, in the lee of the headland, was found the
Mycenaean cemetery of Archontikí (50 mins), first excavated in 1962. It is from here that the remarkably rich
finds exhibited on the upper floor in the Archaeological
Museum of Chios were rescued. The curving sweep of
the bay, the off-shore islets, the protecting headland to
north, and the small area of what must once have been
cultivable land, explain the reasons for settlement here,
combined with the fact that this bay represents one of
the first landfalls for boats making the hazardous crossing from west to east across the open waters of the central Aegean on the early trade routes to Asia Minor and
the Black Sea.

More than 50 Mycenaean graves (14th–12th centuries BC),
cut relatively deeply and built with split slabs of stone, have
now been investigated. They are visible from the shore-side
perimeter fence at the northern end of the area. Many of the
graves were rescued from erosion by the sea. The **funerary
offerings** found in the graves give a vivid sense of the importance and wealth of the Bronze Age settlement here, suggesting that this was a vibrant trading *emporion*. The finds

include a wide variety of decorated ceramic objects (of both male and female appurtenance), bronze swords and daggers, seal-stones, and several kinds of metal and glass-paste jewellery of fine workmanship and attractively delicate colour. As excavations progress the same richness of objects continues to be found. The settlement itself, which reveals commensurately spacious houses with storage areas and *pithoi* still *in situ*, has so far been only partially explored. The Archontikí area continued to be inhabited into early historic times, during which there is evidence from ceramic offering-cups of the cult of an (as yet) unidentified hero.

Regaining the main road and continuing north, you come to a small, white memorial stone by a junction leading down to the attractive **bay of Ftelió**. This marks the spot where, on 21 June 1824, a large number of the local population perished—either by communal suicide or by accident—when the island's powder magazine to which they had taken refuge was exploded. The valley of Ftelió has surface water and there are welcome beds of reeds and a few trees behind the long and pleasant sandy beach.

From Ftelió the road climbs continuously for a further hour across the northern side of the island as far as the monastery. At the crown of the first ridge a tiny

settlement is seen below, marked by three relatively recent churches whose type of construction is peculiarly
characteristic of the island. The central dome is low and
broad, and its curve soon inverts and turns convex in a
low sweep to the shoulders, giving the buildings more the
profile of an Ottoman mosque. This design is repeated in
other rural churches on the island. As the road begins to
climb more steeply, you pass to the left the abandoned
settlement of **Xerókambos** where older stone houses and
evidence of terracing lie in ruins. Finds from a Roman
installation and a late Roman cemetery have been made
here.

The road climbs further and terminates just as the
north coast of Chios comes into view at the **monastery of
the Koimisis tis Theotokou** (Dormition of the Virgin), a
fine and compact ensemble of buildings in a magnificent
position on the shoulder of Mount Prophitis Elias. The
founding of the monastery is thought to date from the
15th or 16th century, although exact historical documen-
tation is lacking. Most of the fabric was rebuilt after the
Turkish destruction of 1824, but the form remains faith-
ful to the pre-existing design. The spacious *catholicon*,
preceded by a domed narthex, has an octagonal drum
and cupola supported on three conches: there are no
wall-paintings in the interior. The monastery celebrates

on 1 August, when the islanders process hither with a sacred icon of the Virgin. It was left uninhabited in 1983; since when the buildings have been sensitively restored and conserved. (*The key is kept by the island's pappás, who can normally be found around the promenade area of the harbour in the evening.*)

PRACTICAL INFORMATION

82 104 Psará: area 40 sq. km; perimeter 45km; resident population 478; max. altitude 531m. **Port Authority**: Chios, T. 22710 44433. **Information**: T. 22740 61293.

ACCESS

Access is effectively only from Chios, apart from one weekly ferry which comes up from Lavrion (for Athens) on Mondays on it way to Lesbos (Sigri), Aghios Efstratios and Lemnos and returns down the same line on Wednesdays. The most regular connection is the **F/B Nisos Thira** (**NEL Lines**: T. 22710 43981, fax 41443) which leaves Psará every morning for Chios, except Tuesdays, and returns in the afternoon (4hrs). During the summer months only, there is a caïque service from Limniá (Volissos) on the west coast of Chios which crosses to Psará on Saturdays and returns on Sundays (90mins.). Once on the island, transportation is very limited: there is no taxi or vehicle rental of any sort. If you do not have your own vehicle, it is only possible to explore the island by foot—and there is no roadside shade at any point.

LODGING

Lodging is limited: the choice is either the clean (but quite expensive) **Psará Hotel** (*T. 22740 61180 & 61195*) at the northern extremity of the town; or the **Restalia Studios** (*T. 22740 61000 & 61201*), close to the port, which only operate in July and August.

EATING

There are three tavernas on the island: those on the port promenade serve fairly ordinary fare; substantially better and with a pleasing view is the **Taverna Heliovasilema** ('Sunset') on the town's south beach of Kato Gialos.

GLOSSARY

amphora—a tall, terracotta receptacle with handles for the transportation of liquids

antae (sing. *anta*)—square pilasters or projections which frame an entrance or portico

Archaic period—the 7th and 6th centuries BC

aryballos—a spherical or elongated cylindrical flask with a narrow neck for containing oil or perfume, generally made of pottery but sometimes of alabaster or marble

ashlar—stone masonry which uses large, dressed, regular blocks

breccia—(of marble) a large patch of a different colour from that of the main field of the stone

catholicon—the church at the centre of an Orthodox monastery

cavea—the hemicycle of seats accommodating the public in a theatre

chiton— a woollen or linen item of clothing worn by both men and women in antiquity, rectangular in form, fixed at the shoulders, and draped so as to cover most of the body except the arms

chochlakia—a method of cobble-paving with small,

uniform, rounded, black and white pebbles, often attractively laid in abstract or figurative patterns, especially popular in the Eastern Aegean

crepidoma—the platform of a temple in its entirety, often consisting of three superimposed levels which successively decrease in size

debitage—the discarded material left from the production of chipped stone tools or objects

dentils—the cut, rectangular, teeth-like decorations on the underside of a cornice

entablature—the upper part of an ancient building above the columns (including the architrave, frieze, cornice, etc.)

epigonation—a small, Orthodox liturgical vestment, square in form and highly embroidered

exonarthex—an outer vestibule of a Byzantine church, preceding the narthex (see below)

Geometric period—the 10th–late 8th centuries BC

Hellenistic period—era of, and after, the campaigns of Alexander the Great, c. 330–c. 150 BC

Hosios—'blessed'; the title given to a beatified individual in the Greek Orthodox Church

iconostasis—the high wooden screen (generally holding icons and images) which separates the sanctuary from the main body of an Orthodox church, and which with time came to substitute the masonry *templon* (*see below*) of earlier Byzantine churches

in antis—(of columns) set between projecting side-walls or wings (*antae*) of a building

isodomic—(of masonry) constructed in parallel courses of neatly-cut rectangular blocks

kalderimi—a stone-paved or cobbled pathway or mule-track

kambos—any fertile area near a settlement used for food-cultivation

kore (pl. *korai*)—the statue of a robed, standing female figure, common in Archaic sculpture (cp *kouros* below)

kouros—the statue of a nude, male figure, common in Archaic sculpture

kulliye—the entirety of a complex of religious buildings in Ottoman architecture

kylix—a shallow, wide-bowled (generally decorated) drinking cup with stem, foot and horizontal handles

machicolation—a defensive projection out from a fortified building, often over the entrance or at a corner, from which projectiles or hot liquids could be dropped on assailants

megaron—the great hall of a Mycenaean palace, rectangular in shape and generally preceded by a porch

naos—the central interior area of a Byzantine church or

the inside chamber of a pagan temple

narthex—the entrance vestibule of a Byzantine church, often running the width of the building

orchestra—the circular, or partially circular, floor of a theatre reserved for the chorus and for dance

Pantocrator—the name given in Byzantine art and theology to Christ seen as the all-powerful ruler

parecclesion—a discrete chapel attached and parallel to a larger main church

peribolos—the perimeter wall of a temple precinct

peristyle—a colonnade which encloses an area, a building or a courtyard

phialostomia—hollow terracotta tubes or mouths with crimped sides, immured in the masonry of Byzantine buildings for decorative purposes and to ventilate the walls

pithos (pl. *pithoi*)—a large, tall, ceramic storage jar, sometimes used also for burials

plateia—a town or village square

poros stone—any soft limestone of porous composition used for construction

Proconnesian marble—a white marble, veined with grey, quarried on the island of Proconnesus in the Sea of Marmara

prothesis—the niche or whole (apsidal) chamber to the

north side of the main sanctuary of a Byzantine church, used for preparing the liturgical elements of the Eucharist.

pyrgos—a stone tower

pyxis—a rectangular or cylindrical vessel with a lid, often used in antiquity by women as a box for containing cosmetics

sgraffito—the decorative technique of laying more than one layer of different-coloured plaster on a wall and creating decoration by scratching away the uppermost layer according to a specific design.

spolia—elements and fragments from ancient buildings re-used in later constructions

squinch—similar to pendentives, they are the solid triangles between the four arches that support the rim on which a dome is to be raised; squinches are simpler than pendentives and can sometimes take the form of corner arches or niches

stele (pl. *stelai*)—a carved tablet or grave-stone

stoa—a long, covered colonnade open on one side and closed (by shops or offices) on the other

talus—the reinforced base of a fortification which slopes or swells outwards below the vertical drop of he wall above

Taxiarchis (pl. *Taxiarches*)—Archangel

templon—the stone or masonry screen in a church which closes off the sanctuary

tesserae—the small pieces of coloured stone or glass-paste which compose a mosaic

thesmophoreion—a place for the ritual worship of Demeter, mostly frequented by women

Tourkokratia—the period of Turkish Ottoman dominion in Greece

INDEX

General

Achermos	15
Alcibiades	16
Alexander the Great	17, 41
Apartis, Thanassis	114, 118
Apostolis, Nikolis	154, 157
Argentis, Philip	35
Ariousion wine	111
Boardman, John	81
Breccia di Aleppo, marble	53–54
Byron, Lord	126, 130
Chandler, Richard	31
Chomatzas, Michael	27, 52
Cicero	9, 22
Constantine IX Monomachos	57
Croesus, King of Lydia	15
Delacroix, Eugène	12, 20, 36, 130–131
Demosthenes	153
Dioscorides	87–88
Domestichos, Antonios	92
Eliot, Sir Charles	127, 130
Fraser, Juliette May	49–50

General continued

Giustiniani family	19, 30, 31, 72, 77
Glaucus	15
Glykas, Aristides	143–144
Herodotus	15, 117, 140
Homer	9, 15, 115, 124, 153
Hosref Pasha	154
Ion	15
Kanaris, Constantine	20, 26, 36, 130, 154, 157–158
Kara Ali Pasha	20, 32, 129, 130, 158
Koraïs, Adamantios	35
Lemos family	141, 142, 145
Logothetis, Lycourgos	128
Lyras family	141
Mahmud II	129
Marmor Chium (Portasanta)	22, 34–35
Massacre of Chios, 1822	126–132
Mastic	19, 87–90
Mausolus of Halicarnassus	17
Melik Pasha	27
Papanikolaos, Dimitris	157
Pateras family	36, 141, 142, 145, 146
Pliny	15, 22
Solomos, Dionysios	154
St Isidore	18, 33

General continued

St Paul   18
Strabo   153
Sulla   18
Syngros, Andreas   73
Theocritus   15
Theopompus   15
Thucydides   14, 16, 79, 106, 117
Tiberius   18
Tombros, Michalis   26, 114
Varvakis, Ioannis   154
Verres   17
Victor Hugo   130
Watchtowers on Chios   100–102
Zenobios   17

Chios   **9–136**
Chios town   22–53
Aghia Myrope and Aghios Isidoros,
    church of   33–34
Aghios Giorgios Frouriou, church of   32
Aghios Giorgios 'Ghiázou', church of   49
Aghios Vasílios Petrokókkinon, church of   25–26
Archaeological Museum   37–44
Bayraklı Mosque   32

Chios continued

  Chios town continued

Bazaar	25
Byzantine Museum	27–28
Giustiniani 'Palace'	28–29, 52
Kampos area	44–49
Kastro	29–32
Koraïs Library and Argentis Folklore Museum	33, 35–36, 55
Maritime Museum	36
Mecediye Mosque	27
Ottoman baths	31
Ottoman cemetery	32
Ottoman fountain	27
Panaghia 'Kokoroviliá'	49
Panaghia 'Syriótissa', church of the	49
Plateia Plastíra (Plateia Vounáki)	23
Porta Maggiore	30
'Portasanta' marble-quarries	34–35
Turkish watch-tower	31
Aghia Marina, chapel of, Phaná	93
Aghia Markella, monastery, Limniá	107–108
Aghia Paraskeví, Olýmpi	94
Aghia Paraskeví, Ziphiás	104
Aghiásmata	111–112

Chios continued

Aghii Apostoli, church of the, Pyrgí 91–93
Aghii Pateras, monastery of 67
Aghio Gála 108–110
Aghios Giorgios, church of, Mestá 99
Aghios Giorgios Prastias, Sideroúnta 72
Aghios Giorgios Sikousis 103–104
Aghios Ioannis Argentis, church of 76
Aghios Ioannis, church of, Chalkeío 104–105
Aghios Ioannis, Sideroúnta 72
Aghios Ioannis, village and church 110
Aghios Markos, monastery of 54
Aghios Panteleimon, church of, Mestá 99
Aghios Thalelaios, Aghio Gála 110
Aghios Theodoros, chapel of, Phanai 95, 97
Aípos, mount 123
Amádes 120
Anávatos 68–70, 130
Ano Kardámyla 118
Apolichnes, castle of 76–77
Apollo *Phanaios*, temple of 95–96
Armólia 76
Avgónyma 68, 130
Black Beach 84
Chalkeío 104–105

Chios continued

Dievchá	122
Dótia, tower of	84–85
Elata	102
Elinda, bay of	71
Emporeió	78
Emporeios, ancient	78–84
Genoese castle, Volissos	106
Great Tower, Pyrgí	91
Grías Castle, Kardámyla	118
Homer's Rock (*Daskalópetra*), Vrontados	115–116
Kalamotí	77
Kambiá	120
Kardámyla	117–118
Karyés	53
Katarráktis	75–76
Kidianta	117
Koimisis tis Theotokou, church of the, Pyrgí	91
Kómi	78
Kouroúnia	111
Langáda	116–117
Limniá	106
Lithí	72–73
Livadíou watchtower	100
Margaritis, peninsula	118–119

Chios continued

Mármaro   118
Mastic villages and groves   85–105
Megali Vigla   119
Melaniós   108
Merikounta Bay   100
Mestá   97–100
Moni Moundón (Aghios Ioannis Prodromos),
    monastery of, Dievcha   121–123
Nagos   119–120
Nea Moni   54–67
Olýmpi   93–94
Olýmpi Cave   94–95
Oria, castle of   121
Palaeochristian basilica, Emporeio   83
Palaio Katarráktis   76
Paliá Potamiá   112
Panaghia Aghiogalousena,
    church of the, Aghio Gála   109
Panaghia Agrelopoúsena, church of the,
    Kalamotí   77–78
Panaghia, church of the, Kambiá   121
Panaghia Krina, church of the   28, 51–52
Panaghia Rouchouniótissa, convent of the,
    Katarráktis   76

Chios continued

Panaghia Sikeliá, monastery of the	75
Pelinnaion, mount	121
Phanai, ancient	95
Phokí, bay of	84
Pitiós	124
Pyrgí	90–93
Rimókastro	124–125
Sideroúnta	71–72
Sklaviá	52
Spartounda	121
St Anne, chapel of, Aghio Gála	109
Ta Markou	113
Taxiarches, church of the, Mestá	98–99
Taxiarches, church of the, Olýmpi	94
Taxiarches, old church of the, Mestá	99
Tigáni	71
Trachíli	71
Vavíli	49–50
Véssa	102–103
Víki	120, 121
Volissos	106–108
Vrontados	114
Vroulídia Bay	119
Ypapanti, chapel of the, Vavíli	49–50

Chios continued
    Ziphiás   104

Oinousses   **137–149**
    Aghios Nikolaos, church of, Aignousa   144
    Aignousa   142–145
    Análipsi, church of the   145
    Annunciation of the Virgin, convent of the 145–146
    Maritime Museum, Aignousa   142–144
    Voutyro   146

Psará   **150–165**
    Aghia Anna and Aghios Ioannis, church of   155–156
    Aghia Paraskevi, church of   159
    Aghios Nikolaos, church of   156
    Archontikí, Mycenaean cemetery   160–161
    Ftelió, bay of   161
    Koimisis tis Theotokou, monastery of   162–163
    Limnos Bay   159
    Mávri Ráchi, rock of   155
    Metamorphosis, church of the   158
    Taxiarchis (and Aghios Spyridon),
        church of the   156–157
    Xerókambos   162